Interiors for

Under 5s

Other Wiley Editorial Offices

John Wiley & Sons Inc., 111 River Street, Hoboken, NJ 07030, USA

Jossey-Bass, 989 Market Street, San Francisco, CA 94103-1741, USA

Wiley-VCH Verlag GmbH, Boschstr. 12, D-69469 Weinheim, Germany

John Wiley & Sons Australia Ltd, 33 Park Road, Milton, Queensland 4064,
Australia

John Wiley & Sons (Asia) Pte Ltd, 2 Clementi Loop #02-01, Jin Xing
Distripark, Singapore 129809

John Wiley & Sons Canada Ltd, 22 Worcester Road, Etobicoke, Ontario,
Canada M9W 1L1

ISBN 0 470 09332 3

Printed and bound by Conti Tipocolor, Italy

Interiors for

Under 5s

International Academy of
Design & Technology
39 John Street
Toronto, Ontario M5V 3G6

Melissa Jones

Series Designer Liz Sephton

can
you
see
the
giant's
legs?

contents

Executive Commissioning Editor: Helen Castle
Editorial and Design Management: Mariangela Palazzi-Williams
Editorial Assistance: Famida Rasheed

Photographic Credits

Cover: © Richard Davies

pp 2–3, 21 & 114–9 © Bremner & Orr Design/Ray Rathborne; pp 1, 109 & 112–3 © Bremner & Orr Design Consultants; pp 4(t), 82–3, 87 & 102–7 © Daisy Hutchison; pp 4(b), 44–9, 71–9 & 191 © Behnisch, Behnisch & Partner, photographer: Christian Karndzie; pp 5(t) & 120–3 Photos: Denis Finnin © American Museum of Natural History (AMNH); pp 5(b) & 195–7 © Todhunter Earle Interiors; pp 7, 11, 127, 162–3, 165 & 190 PhotoDisc, Inc.; p 8 Mary Evans Picture Library; pp 9, 17, 79, 80 & 81(t) © Alsop & Partners, photographer: Alan Lai; pp 10, 12(l), 85 & 164 © The Natural History Museum, London; p 12(r) Victoria & Albert Museum/V&A Images; pp 13 & 40–3 © Martine Hamilton Knight/Built Vision; pp 14–5 & 22–5 © Tim Soar; p 16 Mary Evans/Henry Grant; p 18 © Future Systems; pp 19, 129 & 153–5 © Future Systems, photographer: Soren Aagaard; p 20 © jmarchitects; pp 26–33 © Rob t' Hart; pp 34–5 © Joan Rodon Arquitectes Associats; pp 36–9 & 93–4 © Helene Binet; pp 50–7, 78 & 81(b) © Alsop & Partners, photographer: Roderick Coyne; pp 59 & 61 © Gans & Jelacic; p 60 © Gans & Jelacic, photographer: Francesca Phister; pp 62–9 © Dennis Gilbert/VIEW; p 84 © Science Museum; pp 86 & 89–91 © Science Museum/Tim Hawkins; p 95 Victoria & Albert Museum/Museum of Childhood at Bethnal Green; pp 97–9 © Benedict Luxmore/arcaid.co.uk; pp 100 & 101(b) © Jeff Goldberg/Esto; p 101(t) © Ralph Richter/Esto; p 110 © Jan Baldwin; p 111 © Buckinghamshire County Museum; pp 124–5 & 135–7 © Denise Ho Architects; p 128 © John Haworth, photo: Alan Williams; pp 130–3 © A R Hagdrup; pp 138–9 © Hotel Tresanton Ltd; pp 140–5 © Stephen Gage; pp 146–9 © Tom Scott; pp 150–2 & 192 © Richard Davies; pp 156–9 © R B Fisher; pp 160–1 © The London Aquarium BV; pp 166–171 © Atelier Suda; pp 172–3 © Soho House; pp 174–5 Ian Lambot; pp 176–7 © Hufton and Crow; pp 178–181 © Stacey Mutkin; pp 182–3, 186–7 & 198–9 © Richard Bryant/arcaid.co.uk; p 184 © Hull News & Pictures; p 185 © Lorne Capmbell; pp 188–9 & 206–211 © Michaelis Boyd Associates, photographer: Richard Lewisohn; p 193 courtesy of Laura Ashley at PRshots; pp 201–5 © Hopkins Architects.
Picture research for images on pages 1, 8, 16, 18–20, 108–113, 128–9, 150, 153, 165(b) & 192–3 by Mariangela Palazzi-Williams.

'Home is where one starts from.'
TS Eliot, Four Quartets, 'East Coker', v, 190

Home. Our first world. The interiors that give us our first sounds, sights and smells are the most important places we will ever inhabit. They shape us, and by doing so take root indelibly in our minds and the structure of our cells. The years from birth to five are the years that form us, providing the blueprint for who we are.

When you think of architecture, it is most often of cathedrals and castles and public buildings for adult sensibilities. These can certainly be visited by

Introduction

young children, and form part of their experience of the world. But equally important, if not more so, are the buildings we first see and become accustomed to, and inhabit day to day. They show us what to expect from our brave new world. This first world, the starting point, is being given more attention than ever before by architects and designers.

Earliest sense memories are so intensely embedded in us that they can be triggered by chance reminder throughout our adult lives. I remember my first bedroom – going to bed when it was still light, the evening sunlight coming through the crimson curtains and making them burnished and glowing and beautiful. That and the wallpaper next to my bed of orange and pink flowers that I would gaze at before falling asleep. When we are very young the world is so strange and new, experienced with no barrier between senses and self. But the subconsciously recorded world is equally as potent as the world of the immediate senses.

Below: This little boy is concentrating on expressing himself with paint with the total absorption characteristic of children. Aided by the light from outside, this interior is sympathetic to creativity.

The other form of interior for children, also so close to home, are the pictures in a storybook, and the first words that go with them. The influence of that concentration of childhood's gaze, homing in on a close-up world, the eye caught by an image there on the page, fantasy stimulated forever, cannot be overemphasised. First stories are worlds made of words, the nursery rhymes full of danger and comedy and good and evil. And a bit later there are the more complicated imaginary worlds of myth, like those featured in *The Lion the Witch and the Wardrobe*, *Peter Pan* and *Harry Potter*.

There is also the world of the cartoon – its characters bouncing through space, impervious, hysterical, immortal – a universe both violent and appealing. Disney has done more to create a unified childhood universe, harnessing and taming infant fears and longings into full length features, building its own illusory interiors in Florida, California and Paris, than any childhood theorist I can think of. It has packaged childhood with its own brand and parents can literally buy into that identity for their children.

Below: This watercolour of a nineteenth-century French nursery provides an idyllic image of children in harmony with their well-proportioned, ordered and calm interior.

Right: The surroundings might change, but group activities and story-telling remain a central theme in the teaching of young children – as here at Alsop & Partners' Fawood Children's Centre at the Stonebridge Estate in London.

Yet invisible interiors existed long before Disney or the current fashion for designing for children. When children fitted into adult interiors they maintained their own powerful childish interior world quite independent of the material world around them. For many, the imagination was the principal dwelling place.

The Victorian nursery or children's quarters were in many ways better suited to children – at least for the well-off – than are domestic interiors today. To begin with, there was much more space. Middle- and upper-class children had their own suites of rooms, sometimes their own floor, presided over by Nanny and including schoolroom as well as playroom and bedroom. Looking back across the centuries, such a separation from their parents is now regarded as a bad thing for children. While in the past there was a lack of intimacy within families, there was often a principal carer, which is not the case for many children now in childcare facilities outside the home. Of course, extra space and the separate childhood world can work both ways. Many children remember an idyll, others confinement and too much discipline. Certainly, childhood itself extended well into teenage years, with no concept of an adolescent culture, let alone a childhood one.

Now children's interiors are approached in a different way. Buildings outside the home are providing for more and more young children. With a greater proportion of working parents, there are more facilities for early years' childcare and education. At weekends families want to go out and about together and

spend time in environments that have something for everyone. So now there are hotels with children's playrooms and facilities, child-friendly restaurants, swimming pools and shops. Museums are putting enormous effort into attracting children – helping them to experience and participate in art and science from an early age. Childcare facilities and nursery schools are concentrating on encouraging educators to work alongside architects to design the best possible spaces – both for the imagination and for practical needs.

We are questioning how we want our children to enter the world. As well as optimism, we want to bring light, space and order into children's lives and there is the desire to keep them safe. Children don't play on the street the way they used to. They no longer roam freely and explore the world through their senses. Contemporary interiors are often substitutes for nature, and as a way of avoiding inactivity and the television, parents seek to stimulate their children and care for them in a controlled way.

'If a child is not allowed to be a child he will remain a child.' This idea is uppermost in our thinking, to allow room for childhood, to make space for it. With the world facing so many challenges which adults often find unbearable, there is greater emphasis than ever on letting children be free to imagine and to express themselves before becoming adults. And we want them to feel safe. Some theorists have felt that there can be too much pressure on children to provide the magic for parents that has gone from their own lives. As we plan our children's delights I think there is an element of that yearning for lost innocence and magic, and it comes as a legacy of the industrial revolution when thinkers first began to examine childhood as a concept.

This concept – childhood – did not fully emerge until society moved from the feudal, land based structure to the industrial. Children were taken off the land they had worked or lived on for centuries and many went to work in factories and inhabited the tenements of the first industrial cities. The first kindergartens – the word has all the overtones of a replacement Eden – were in many ways places of refuge for traumatised children, psychologically exhausted and physically weakened by the privations of city living. With such exploitation of children came a parallel sentimentalising of childhood that we see in the work of Dickens, a need to elevate the condition of innocence and celebrate it with one hand, while taking it away with the other. (And who could forget the child's interior world of the Red Room into which Jane Eyre is locked and which symbolises her rage?)

Right: Discovery: the delight of finding the starfish, connecting with them, concentrating on that one thing – seeing an echo in the shape of her own hands. To recreate these conditions in an interior is a great challenge.

Now that, for the Western world at least, childhood has been returned to the child, the focus has continued to grow on the best way to nurture and provide for our young.

However we look at childhood, there is always, I think, a sense of loss. In her Journals, Sylvia Plath talks of 'the lovely never-never land of magic . . . of little princes and their rose bushes, of poignant bears and Eyore-ish donkeys, of life personalised as the pagans loved it, of the magic wand, and the faultless illustrations – the beautiful dark-haired child . . . winging through the midnight sky on a star-path in her mother's box of reels, – of Griselda in her feather-cloak, walking barefoot with the Cuckoo in the lantern-lit world of nodding Mandarins, – of Delight in her flower-garden with the slim-limbed flower sprites, – of the Hobbit and the Dwarves, gold-belted with blue and purple hoods, drinking ale and singing of dragons in the caverns of the valley — all this I knew and felt and believed. All this was my life when I was young. To go from this to the world of 'grown-up' reality . . .' She doesn't complete the thought, but we can infer how hard she felt that adjustment to be. Along with this loss is the need to replace, to replenish, to give our children what we no longer have, and to enjoy it with them, to vanquish our own sense of passing time.

At the beginning of the 21st century I think we are aware of our vulnerability – and the planet's – in a new way. To concentrate on preparing our children for the world in the most positive way possible has to be a very good thing. And sensitivity to what a child responds to is very important. Yet there is still no easy answer to what makes a successful interior for a young child. When my son was a baby, he used to be filled with quiet awe whenever I took him to a church or cathedral, or indeed any large space. Now he's old enough to walk (or run) around a church he enjoys a feeling of great freedom and delight. Babies and children don't always need to feel in control of the scale of a space, or need delineation and strong colour. They are equally happy with the amorphous: they love looking into the vastness of the sky, or at water running from a tap, or at the sea. After all, they are creatures like adults, only less formed, almost amphibious. They have an aesthetic sense, and the same need for peace as we do. So I think it's important to avoid being too prescriptive. The interiors in this book allow for the child to contribute to the space, to complete it by their presence.

Children are also immensely secretive, and private spaces are important. The closest a little child comes to designing its own interior is making a house

Below: Lunch room at the V&A, used for children's activity days. While neither built nor designed with young children in mind, this well lit, well ventilated and generous space combines with its system of trestle tables and felt pinboards to provide the ideal backdrop for calm, industrious fun.

Left: The tables and seating in the basement lunchroom in London's Natural History Museum create a colourful and sculptural focus in a historic setting. They provide the pleasures generally associated with cafe and restaurant dining to those families who bring their own refreshments.

Above: Outdoor space is as important for children as indoor space. The Hoyle Early Years Centre in Bury, designed by dsdha (Deborah Saunt David Hill Architects), provides children with disabilities with nursery care in a meadow-like setting.

underneath a table with a blanket or sheet, filling it with cushions, toys and private treasures and feeling it is their kingdom. There is a yearning even in the very young for a hidden, private world. Within that world stories are spun and games are played: special friends allowed in, others turned away, surprise attacks mounted, and the child appears and disappears according to his or her own will and nobody else's. So the best children's interiors allow children to use them in their own way.

Outside, children respond very strongly to a vista in a formal garden. They run towards a focal point, and then want to find a way round it, discover a secret place. This human need for a journey through space and a revealed destination is the starting point of the classical garden, and it can be incorporated into an interior for a child with a little thought, and if conditions are right.

It takes imagination, dedication, patience, a sense of fun and, above all, love to bring up children. And it is tremendously exciting that so much thought is now going in to designing for children. After all, our first world is a vulnerable one. These interiors are an expression of the inner foundations we as adults want to provide for our children, so that their start in life can be the firmest, the most positive. We are treasuring them through these spaces. In the end it is the intangibles – love, respect and nurturing – that are the most important. These interiors are manifestations of those feelings. In these exciting designs our hopes and love for our children are made real.

LEARNING

There is a plethora of theories about early childhood education but very little consensus or collaboration between architects and teachers.

In the 21st century educators and architects are joining forces, but up until now design has not been informed by theory. The popularity of a more broadly based approach does not mean, though, that all new interiors are the

Learning

same: while some are simple and practical, others are quirky and full of humour and inventiveness. And once again that is influenced by how adults perceive the children they are designing for.

In the 18th century Rousseau espoused the doctrine of the pure essential Man, and his ideas about education were based mainly on the importance of a spiritual communion with nature. Recreating paradise lost was his preoccupation. For him the child was a unique individual with no preconceptions – a blank slate. In propounding theories about childhood he

Left: In this 1960s Italian nursery, the surroundings were sanitised and regimented. Children were organised and confined in their playpens and staff were dressed in professional nurses' uniforms. This contrasts greatly with the thought and imagination that is put into creating today's warm and child friendly environments, making their first contact with 'learning' full of fun and enjoyment.

Above: This contemporary nursery, designed by Alsop & Partners for the Fawood Children's Centre, London, demonstrates how space for play can be organised in an open and unconfined way. Children are able to pursue different activities without the interior being subdivided.

was followed by Froebel, who trained as an architect and invented the concept of the kindergarten. He was fascinated by three shapes – the cone, the square and the triangle – and believed that a child need not and could not learn to draw from nature until he had mastered these basic forms.

In the 19th century theories on childhood learning took a more pragmatic turn. While there were the cruel corrective institutions described by the Bröntes and Dickens, there were also the first kindergartens founded by Robert Owen in the north of England and Margaret Macmillan in London. Owen's was Britain's first nursery, founded in 1816 at New Lanark. Light and airy with a musicians' gallery, it was the school that supported the workers at his factory. Owen believed that children learn from direct experience – he once encouraged a teacher to bring a live crocodile into the school for the children to observe. He was a firm believer in fresh air and exercise – the school was held outside in good weather and, weather permitting, there was always three hours a day of free play in the open playground. Order, kindness, cleanliness were taught, as well as singing, dancing, marching and basic

geography. Owen eventually presided over three schools: for ages two to four, four to six and from seven upwards. On the walls were paintings, maps and natural objects. In London Margaret Macmillan pioneered a nursery with garden to allow for free movement and play, providing a haven for many children of the industrial revolution in the slums of Deptford. In 1928 she said, 'The school of tomorrow will be a garden city for children'.

The 20th century saw Maria Montessori's approach take precedence. She valued simplicity: training for independence, learning through touch, practical skills. The autonomy of the child, its dignity, was paramount. But after the Second World War there was a swing back towards the home, which has only recently been reversed.

And then there is the visionary approach. Having just read Le Corbusier's booklet about the nursery at the Unité d'Habitation in Marseilles in the 1950s, I have been immensely moved. The school took up one floor of this huge concrete tower city. The children sat on the floor, learned from blackboards and wheeled free-standing furniture around. Inset into the walls were shelves housing their work that looked like recesses for icons in a catholic church. Grilles covered balconies with views to the mountains. A concrete ramp led to a vast sky garden complete with lavender, a slope for running down and a

Above: This 'Classroom of the Future' was designed in 2001 by Future Systems; the architects best known for their innovative Media Centre at Lords and landmark building for Selfridges in Birmingham. The office is interested in the possibilities for pre-fabricated learning spaces in inspired and creative forms, which incorporate new technologies.

Above: Future Systems have produced two classrooms for schools in the Borough of Richmond, Southwest London-Meadlands primary school and Grey Court secondary school. At a time when there is a shortage in nursery provision, investment in flexible and well-developed designs that can be manufactured offsite seems like an important option for the under fives.

paddling pool. The children look full of joy, even while their environment was pronounced unsafe by those whom Le Corbusier saw as reactionary. It is hard to imagine such a school being built today, but it must be remembered for its imaginative approach and the strength of the community it accommodated.

Back to reality – and the 21st century. There is still an incoherent approach to education across the developed world. In Britain and United States children go to nursery from nought to five. In Scandinavia it is seven, in other European countries six. It is agreed that infants up to 20 months should have their own space. In Japan, over 85 per cent of over threes attend kindergarten, of which 25 per cent are state maintained. Private schools charge up to one third of parents' income. In France the state funds 95 per cent of learning facilities for three to five year olds. Spain is moving towards free care for three to fives. In Italy, 90 per cent of that age group attend full time state funded nursery. They have introduced a constitution of children's rights and a multidisciplinary approach whereby local councillors join architects and child educationalists in planning a school. In Denmark, 65 per cent of three year olds are in state funded education. Compare this to the UK, where only 41 per cent of three year olds go to part time nursery and there is a continuing confusion among kindergarten, nursery school and pre-school.

The new Sure Start initiative is putting £250m into kick-starting an early years development plan, designating some schools Early Excellence Centres to provide inspiration. The UK is attempting to narrow the gap between its provision and that of the rest of Europe.

So, what should these schools that cater for the early years be providing? Physical exercise is a key component. As children's lives are now so ordered and confined, there needs to be room for them to run around, fall over, climb, touch, find out the limitations of their bodies, develop coordination and so learn and grow. A nursery needs to provide an outdoor space that is safe, light, airy, stimulating and calm. Indoors, the interior needs to take into account the sight lines and scale requirements of the young child. The space needs to be divided for different activities, so it has to be flexible. There has to be plenty of accessible storage, locker, washing and bathroom facilities the children can find easily and manage by themselves. After that it is about the teachers and children – how they forge a community that is loving, ordered, open.

The interiors in this chapter are all different. Kleine Kikker is playful on the outside but sensible on the inside. The Jubilee School classrooms give a great sense of ownership, each with their views, outside balcony or terrace, and generous feel. The Swiss school has the great fun element of the built-in furniture, the colours. It has intimacy and warmth. The Migrant Centre, scooped out of a basement and a space beneath the pavement is like a bright cave, welcoming and fun to explore. The Hoyle Nursery provides for children with and without learning disabilities, in a clean, safe way. Peckham library manages to be a reading room and a climbing frame at the same time. And the workbox desk from New York builds a new connection between a child and their desk – transforming it into simultaneous mobile toy and learning device that is truly innovative. The Jigsaw Nursery is a day nursery facility, and its architects have thought hard about the use of space in a varied and interesting way. Finally there is Munster Kindergarten, with its facilities for all day stays, an environment that draws more on the home for its inspiration.

While being very contemporary, each of these interiors has a design heritage that can be traced to domestic or public interiors, a distinct atmosphere it sets out to recreate or challenge; and it is very interesting to see their solutions.

Above: The expanding need for childcare provision has led to imaginative refurbishments of other building types, such as this former MG garage in Richmond, Surrey, which is now occupied by a Happy Times nursery designed by jmarchitects.

Opposite: The entrance to the Discover Children's Centre in East London, designed by Bremner & Orr, evokes a sense of wonder from the outset.

Jubilee School, Tulse Hill, London

AHMM Ltd

Client: Lambeth Council
Completion Date: 2003

The award-winning Jubilee School in Tulse Hill, South London, reaches out into its community, providing nursery school and creche facilities with great thought and attention to detail, and a feeling of lightness, openness and space

The Jubilee School is set in the middle of a housing estate in one of London's most deprived areas. The winner of numerous awards, it benefits from the government's Sure Start initiative – aiming to provide its community with a focus, a positive jumping off point for the future.

The school incorporates an all day créche facility for the under fours, as well as a nursery school that is part of the main primary school. From the outside the building is imposing but approachable, boasting a large outside deck – a bit like a ship's foredeck – that leads into a vast hall that the whole school can assemble in with ease. The outside play areas surrounding the building are graduated; their different levels intended to be less intimidating for young children.

The main classroom wing of the school is designed so that each classroom has its own door to its private outside space – a terrace for the ground floor, verandah for the first floor. Each classroom has almost a wall of glass with views onto the outside. Detailing is precise – the worktop counters where the children leave their art materials have been made out of recycled plastic from coloured cups. This unusual material gives a great sense of colour and play to the rooms.

The nursery classrooms are at ground level, as is the créche – which is just one big space open to the outside on two sides. Here there is a feeling of lightness and a positive outlook. Off the main créche space are bathrooms, changing facilities, a relaxing room with sofas, a little room for cots, and a meeting room where parenting classes are held. This one space is the meeting place for many lives to connect, and in an area where there had been literally no place to go for parents with young children, it is vital. Just as importantly it is designed to a high standard – something perhaps expected in countries like Norway and Sweden, where environments for the very young are well-funded and designed with thought and loving care, but here in the UK it really feels like something special. Building for the future, in this case, has made wishes comes true.

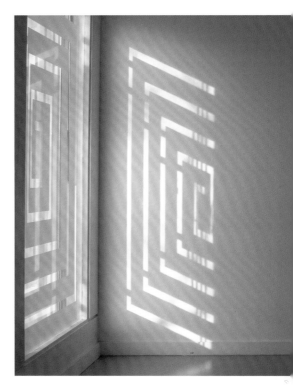

Above: **Jubilee School, London.** This elegant detailing is simple and graceful

Opposite: **Jubilee School, London.** The classroom, flooded with natural light and with plenty of room to work and play

Below: **Jubilee School, London.** The cloakroom at
the creche: simple, practical and pretty

Left: De Kleine Kikker Day Care Centre, Utrecht.
The exterior – like a cross between a funnel and a
letterbox. The mass of the building, the first floor,
appears to float above the ground floor

**Below: De Kleine Kikker Day Care Centre,
Utrecht.** The child's naïve drawing of a house
come to life

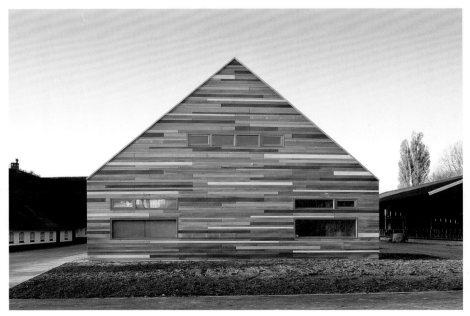

Above: **De Kleine Kikker Day Care Centre, Utrecht.** The colours of the building's wood against the cold sky are beautiful – and give it warmth

Above: **De Kleine Kikker Day Care Centre.** The gorgeous colours of the wood seem framed by the windows, rather than the other way round

Above: De Kleine Kikker Day Care Centre, Utrecht. Asymmetry creates an intimate space for babies and the very young

Right: **De Kleine Kikker Day Care Centre, Utrecht.** The first-floor balcony at the rear of the building provides an outdoor space that is both sheltered and safe

Swiss School Kindergarten, Barcelona, Spain

Joan Rodon Arquitectes Associats
(Collaborators: Anna Fornt, interior designer)

Client: Fundación Escuela Suiza.
Completion Date: October 1997

It isn't a big space but so much has been done to make it beautiful and tangible. The colours are wonderful and there's so much to delight a child in the storage mezzanine cum work and play structure. It makes it fun to go to school, and satisfies a child's sense of order and anarchy all in one.

The kindergarten is on the ground floor of the Swiss School in a residential street in Barcelona. It houses three classrooms. The plan is a basic rectangle with two façades looking onto the street and with an internal patio, for light and ventilation.

The main entrance leads into a vestibule, which also functions as a waiting room, and adjacent to the vestibule, separated by a translucent glass partition is a small office for parent-teacher meetings. Past the vestibule is the service zone composed of bathrooms, changing room and installation spaces.

A long hall connects to the classrooms and contains benches and cubicles for the children to change into their robes and leave their bags. Light pours into the hallway through big glass openings from the classrooms.

Each classroom houses a wet zone, with a washbasin and lavatories for children, and a small wooden mezzanine with storage spaces underneath and a play house on top. All three classrooms open onto the patio through sliding glass doors with a sunshade above, giving a generous feeling of space.

What I like best about the design – apart from the beautiful hallway – is the wooden mezzanine for play and storage. It looks as much fun as a climbing frame but is also very practical. The idea of work and play being part of the same ethos is great.

The earth colours are beautiful, making the rooms feel very specifically Spanish.

Above: Swiss School Kindergarten, Barcelona. An elegant timber faced exterior with neat drinking fountain, and friendly pink floor. A comfortingly chunky façade

Opposite: Swiss School Kindergarten, Barcelona. This classroom structure looks like a cross between a climbing frame and a secret hiding place. The colours are unusual and resonant, mysterious and fun

Créche, Migrants Resource Centre, Pimlico, London

Adams & Sutherland

Client: Migrants Resource Centre, London
Completion Date: 2002

A child's world created out of the basement of a nineteenth-century house in the centre of London. This cosy space, receiving children only for a few hours at a time, has immediate appeal. It is welcoming bright and fun.

The Migrants Resource Centre – a registered charity – is in a dilapidated flat-fronted Victorian house in Pimlico, in a street full of peeling houses, delicatessen and antique shops abutting a red-brick housing estate built in the 1970s.

On a tiny budget, the architects have converted the front of the basement and scooped out some space from under the pavement in front of it to create a welcoming space for children to spend a couple of hours while their parents take English language classes or avail themselves of the advice and support the centre has to offer.

The main space houses a little plastic play house. Off it to the left is a dark and cosy cot room for naps. Straight ahead there are two entrances to the narrow strip which is lit by glass bricks forming the pavement above. Off this strip is a home room, where there is a dresser and toys for domestic play, and a little bathroom equipped with tiny lavatories and basin. The thick wall that supports the front of the building and divides the play space from the bright strip has four holes in its considerable thickness. They look like holes in a piece of cheese, and are great fun to peer into and play around. The narrow pavement part of the space is decorated with a happy animal mural.

It is a clever interior because it is so small and yet it has an element of discovery and surprise. To move through and enjoy the play of light from the pavement above is great fun, and the underground rooms, catacomb like, are tremendously cosy.

The main space is connected to the other basement space via folding doors and a stable half door. The folding doors can be opened to make a big space for meetings, parties, and functions.

The vibrant feeling of this little space is very pleasing, it gives an atmosphere of welcome and shelter and so reflects the aims of the centre itself.

Opposite: **Migrants Resource Centre, London.**
This little passage connects the two underpavement spaces with the main room

Above: **Migrants Resource Centre, London.** Here are the pretty holes the children love to stick their hands through. They also provide shafts of light to the main room

Opposite: **Migrants Resource Centre, London.** The view back from the domestic corner into the main space – both bright and white and warm and orange at the same time

Hoyle Early Years Centre, Bury, Lancashire

dsdha (Deborah Saunt David Hills Architects)

Client: Bury Education Services
Completion Date: 2003

Within a small overall space the architects have created a nursery to accommodate the needs of children, children with disabilities, and their parents and carers – producing a design that looks stylistically unconventional but works very well, closely following the maxim for all good modernists: form follows function.

The Hoyle Early Years Centre in Bury was one of three winning designs in the 2001 Neighbourhood Nurseries Initiatives design competition held by the Department for Education and Skills (DFES) and CABE in 2001. Its aim was to build buildings that were adaptable, functional and inspirational to children. Demands were high for a low budget and a small space. Children with special needs were to be provided for, as well as activities for parents and a focus for

Below: **Hoyle Early Years Centre, Bury.** The outdoor play area is tactile, low maintenance and safe

Above: **Hoyle Early Years Centre, Bury.** The building reaches out into the landscape, illuminating it and providing different degrees of enclosed exterior space

a community with a high level of deprivation. So great has been its success that the new building has been adopted as an exemplar by the Sure Start Children's centre initiative and by CABE.

It has fulfilled the brief: The nursery accommodates 52 children between 2 and 5 years, including 22 with special needs, who mainly come from the surrounding area, although special needs children come from across the borough. Courses are also offered to parents, featuring parenting skills, a family learning project, cookery and crafts along with visiting speakers. The Centre is designated a Resourced Provision School for Children with Communication Difficulties, pointing up its role with special needs.

Aesthetically the building combines a certain clumsy simplicity with a strange kind of elegance. The requirements of the building have dictated its form to produce a design that feels almost naïve.

The building needed natural light, so the steel hangar-like frame lifts the overhanging metal roof above the tops of the original walls, and the newly gained space is infilled with clerestory windows. This floods the building with high light, and combined with the many windows at toddler horizon height, makes a strange but pleasing effect. There seem to be few windows where you would expect them to be. Under-floor heating runs throughout, as much of the children's time is spent on the floor often in bare feet.

According to the Head Teacher, the building is, 'super. It is light and airy, the total opposite of the previous building,' and well suited to its function. Metal screens protecting the entrance form a filigree and have a transparency to allow a generous relationship between the nursery and the street, yet provide extremely robust security to ensure that the building and play areas do not suffer from vandalism.

The interior finishes of all rooms are deliberately simple, allowing for the children's work and teacher's themes to be displayed around the building.

The design cleverly gives an illusion of space; at a recent OFSTED inspection it was remarked how small the spaces really were, but how very well they worked. In summer, sliding doors to the courtyard and to soft external play areas are opened adding transparency to the building.

The building is very much a shell-like blank – clean and simple – and you feel that the children and the adults who care for them have filled it with their own learning and play.

Below: **Hoyle Early Years Centre, Bury.** Windows are not where you would expect them to be, yet vistas to the outside are considered and scaled for the small child

Luginsland Kindergarten, Stuttgart, Germany

Behnisch, Behnisch & Partner

Client: Landeshauptstadt Stuttgart
Completion Date: 1990

This inspirational kindergarten ship is the ship of dreams, of the unconscious mind, of play, of the unfettered imagination. It also works brilliantly, being not only beautiful but solid, practical and designed with ample thought as well as spirit.

The architects see location as the key to this piece of shipbuilding. It is set close to gardens, facing the Kernen hilltops, adjoining vineyards and a long uninterrupted sloping hillside.

It also borders an unremarkable residential area composed of single family houses and small apartment blocks, two-storey cubes with pitched roofs. Instead of reinforcing this building pattern and showing children nothing more remarkable than such a building, the architects chose to connect their design to the romance of the landscape and of the interior fantasy landscape of childhood. They wanted something that the children would remember forever, so they becalmed a ship in a sea of hills and fields.

This wonderful inventiveness in the concept is made even more spectacular by the architects' siting of the ship. It is tilting – as if it were sinking, or had run aground, or was simply sailing the hills around it. This stops it from being a mere installation or folly and instead anchors it to the landscape, making it part of it. And it is so wonderfully daring, with its asymmetrical angles and peculiar perspectives.

Once inside, children realise that this tilting is not a trick – the interior also tilts, also plays with perception of the reality of a room, of a space, of a learning environment. Yet for all its revolutionary purpose, and its confusing perspectives, it is a warm, light and friendly interior. Children being as they are, it probably stops being peculiar to them very quickly and just becomes the world that they are used to at kindergarten. The wooden materials, slopes, handrails, and use of natural light all show a careful respect for children and their needs. It is not a mere vanity building but an exercise in inspirational design.

Those who see it either love it or hate it. It is certainly an extraordinary feat of the imagination and one that cannot fail to make an indelible impression on its children.

Above and opposite: **Luginsland Kindergarten, Stuttgart.** The unexpected made real: the kindergarten ship provides an interesting focus in an otherwise unexceptional residential area

Left: Luginsland Kindergarten, Stuttgart.
Inside, the space tilts but remains practical, as
displayed by the lighting, the glass panel in the
door and the handrail

Below: Luginsland Kindergarten, Stuttgart.
Despite its exciting form, the interior exudes a sense
of calm and space through the use of simple solid
planes and plenty of light

Right and below: Luginsland Kindergarten, Stuttgart. The two sides of the Ship's exterior reflect the areas they overlook, with corrugated metal facing onto the main highway and timber towards the residential streets. The uneven facades blend into the natural and hilly landscape

Left: **Peckham Library, London.** Here you can see how the pod sits in the library floor. It looks a bit like a child's idea of a spaceship. The stairs are out of sight behind the glass doors

Above: **Peckham Library, London.** The front façade with its big jutting top and spindly legs happily plays with the idea of the proportions of a conventional building

Above: **Peckham Library, London.** This side view shows how outlandish the library is in its street setting. Delicate and imposing at the same time

Opposite: **Peckham Library, London.** Inside the children's pod, looking back towards its entrance. Just as in a church or cathedral, you are forced to look up

Left: Peckham Library, London. A look at the library from the back – all lit up on a winter's evening. There is so much to delight the young eye: colour and form make it look like a giant illuminated puzzle or a Rubik's cube. It's also a great mixture of transparency and opaque colour, intriguing and mysterious

Below: Peckham Library, London. A winter afternoon look at the glamorous and glowing front façade

Jigsaw Day Nursery, Wandsworth, London

Walters & Cohen

Client: Jigsaw Day Nurseries plc
Completion Date: December 2000

At this nursery the challenge for the architect was how to make different cosy practical spaces out of one big shell – catering for the needs of babies through to five-year-olds in a structured yet fun way.

This nursery forms part of a new development on the river at Wandsworth. The initial unit provided plenty of light, windows and double height spaces but rather a small outside space and that impersonal feeling of a warehouse waiting to be converted. The surroundings are pavement and rows of other – mainly retail – spaces. It is a generous, modern environment, but one that needed a creative approach to make it sympathetic to the under fives.

There's a small reception area with office and buggy storage, then you go through a door and are in the main space. What the architects have done is build a series of box-like interconnected roofed spaces within the main double height space. When you look at it from above, from the staff/parents' mezzanine, it makes much more sense. The design creates lots of little spaces that can be given over to separate activities for small groups of children, without compromising the feeling of space that the overall height gives you.

Separate from this main cube and to one side are the baby area, kitchen, bathroom, and changing room. The baby area divides into sleeping and waking spaces using curtains and sliding doors. There is a central unit in the waking side with a low height counter for making up feeds and bottles. The day part of the nursery allows lots of light through floor-to-ceiling windows and the babies can see out into the main pedestrianised walkway of the development. This would benefit from blinds or curtains I think to control heat and glare – but the concept is bright and light.

There is a fantastic bathroom – very well designed with everything at the right height for small children and planned so that those washing their hands are on one side and those getting in and out of cubicles on the other. It is amazing how many bathrooms for young children are plagued with log-jams and this design cleverly avoids them.

In the toddler area the Rubik's cube aspect of the design comes into play. You can bypass the entire interconnected box via a wide central axis or you can walk through the different spaces. There are plenty of storage units faced with friendly ply and a soft blue colour is used throughout. The intention is to provide flexibility: sliding doors and curtains can open out or enclose them: in reality, it works better for the staff to have dedicated spaces that do not change – from a practical point of view this makes sense.

Playground access is through full height glass doors – stable doors might

Above: Jigsaw Day Nursery, London. The main walkway, showing sliding doors to different spaces, as well as hanging and storage provision

have been better to keep crawling babies and toddlers from getting in a muddle, but it is beautifully open-feeling, with decking and plenty of activity areas outside.

Their nursery is a child's first introduction to public architecture and the architects feel it should be imaginative. The plan was to improve on the old corridor with rooms off it idea. In such a design a child might only experience one room for half a day or even longer at a time. Here the young child can be doing art in the art space, or having quiet time in a quiet corner, and also enjoy moving through the main corridor and looking up at the mezzanine and high roof above. It is fun, and clearly offers a feeling of play and freedom as well as structure.

Left: Jigsaw Day Nursery, London. A view of the main space from the mezzanine. You can see how it has been boxed in and divided

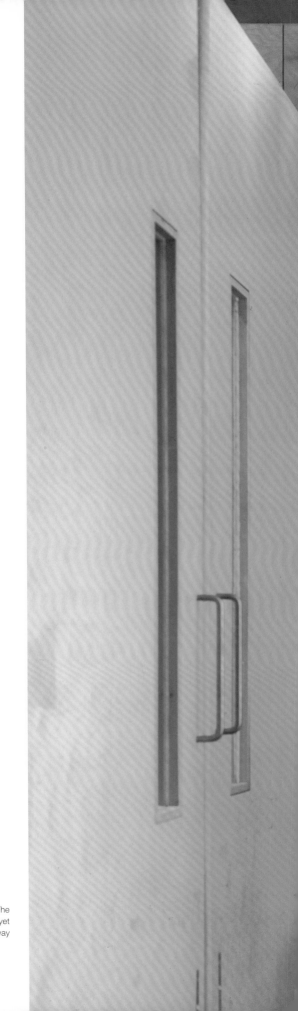

Right: **Jigsaw Day Nursery, London.** The children can do different activities in an open, yet connected way

Above: Jigsaw Day Nursery, London. Upper and lower glazed panels in the doors allow the young to see through as well as the adults

Opposite: Jigsaw Day Nursery, London. Good storage leaves plenty of space for playing

Right: Münster Parish Kindergarten Ingolstadt.
This pretty courtyard is the focus for the school – for
play and for looking at, for peace and for nature

Right: Münster Parish Kindergarten Ingolstadt.
This group 'home' has a very domestic feel. The
wood is warm and homely, and the way the space
is designed with its staircase to the gallery, its kitchen
and activity area, as well asasofa for reading, is very
much like a home, but a home modified for large
groups of children – warm, relaxed and uncluttered

Below: Münster Parish Kindergarten Ingolstadt.
Here you can see how easily accessible the courtyard is from the interior, and how cleverly inside and
outside merge. The atmosphere throughout is cosy,
but the rooms are generous, remaining open and
spacious while providing clearly delineated places
for different activities

Left: Münster Parish Kindergarten Ingolstadt.
View across the courtyard towards two of the three
little houses

Fawood Children's Centre, Stonebridge Estate, London

Alsop & Partners

Client: Stonebridge Housing Action Trust
Completion Date: 2004

With little safe outdoor space available in the centre of cities, an important alternative is expansive interior space. Here Will Alsop and his practice have created a colourful and robust building for young children, which though built economically, is generous in spatial terms.

This innovative building has been constructed rapidly and at low cost to replace an existing children's facility on this large housing estate in Harlesden, north London. It is planned as part of a regeneration project that will involve demolition of surrounding buildings to provide it with a new parkland setting. For now, however, the building provides nursery and play facilities for three- to five-year-olds, including autistic children and those with special needs. In line with the Government's Sure Start initiative, the Centre also provides adult learning services and so is a focal point for its community.

Above: **Fawood Children's Centre, London.** At night, the illuminated exterior is welcoming in its playful use of colour and transparency

Unlike most nurseries, which are long and low with an outdoor space that goes unused in the winter months, the architects have approached designing for the very young in a different way. Theirs is a vast, embellished, decorated and colourful, three-storey, shed-like structure that combines indoor and outdoor spaces under one partly translucent, partly solid roof.

Classrooms are built of reconstituted cargo containers, painted in bright colours and decorated with artwork. These are connected by walkways, balconies, lifts and staircases to the outdoor spaces. Underfloor heating and simple finishes have kept the cost down. The outdoor spaces, or 'outdoor rooms', are all under the same roof.

Opposite: **Fawood Children's Centre, London.** Here the space can be seen in all its triple-height glory. The unobtrusive stage is used at storytime and for drama

Above: **Fawood Children's Centre, London.** The
smaller rooms housed in the containers open directly
on to the large playspace, making the building easy
to navigate and enjoy

Above: **Fawood Children's Centre, London.** A
willow enclosure at one end of the main space can
be explored alone or used for group play

Left: **Fawood Children's Centre, London.**
Depending on the angle, the colourful panels that
adorn the main façade resemble giant pendant ear-
rings or a beaded curtain

ART AND SCIENCE

The way very young children experience museums has changed beyond all recognition. My early memories of going to an exhibition are of hushed voices, silent observation of untouchable exhibits, glass cases, dim lighting, not very friendly smells. There used to be a strong, almost visceral sense of initiation into a grown up world of knowledge, beauty and history, and the feeling that, as children, we were only there on sufferance, that only by paying

Art and Science

proper attention could we earn our stripes, our right to be there. Temples of learning were to be revered.

Now, as a mother taking my own child out and about, so much has changed. For a start, practically every museum or gallery you go to has a special pack aimed at children. So while every institution may not have adapted its spaces – a costly exercise – they are none the less geared to appeal to children, encouraging them to get the most out of what is on show. Children's kits are educational, presented as discovery, and take the form of pointing out special things for them to spot, giving them activities which are

Below: The Children's Gallery at the Science Museum, London, in the 1950s was one of the first to pioneer interactive exhibits.

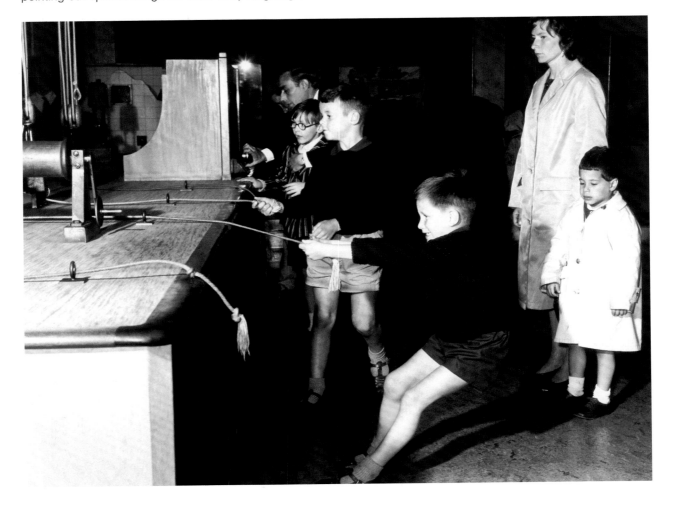

Above: A child is encouraged to discover for herself at the Natural History Museum in London.

creative, such as painting or making something that relates to the current exhibition. There are more parent friendly facilities, particularly children's menus, and the guides to the rooms seem less forbidding and more approachable.

There are old favourites that draw children in: dinosaurs and the great whale at the British Museum, Vikings, any kind of knight and dragon, portraits of people, angels, treasure (the human instinct to collect starts young), swords, mammals, insects, snakes. Tiny minds are particularly drawn to these things and now it is easier than ever to search them out in pictures or behind glass cases.

Those spaces that have gone out of their way to attract children are using bright colours, signs at children's level, and staging special exhibitions just for them, or days full of activities where crowd control is a major skill. There is much more of a feeling of fun, and above all the concept of interactivity: that somehow children can influence or change, certainly participate in, what they are learning by pressing a button, looking at a screen or stimulating something mechanical with their fingertips. Involvement that gives them a sense of achievement.

The pioneer in this revolutionary approach was undoubtedly London's Science Museum. Opened in 1928, it had a children's gallery as early as 1931.

Left: Fantastic colours in the Pattern Pod at London's Science Museum. The child creates the images by moving the chips in and out of the slots in the display panel.

Arriving at the museum is like coming into a vast indoor amusement park, with its huge installations, bright colours, stimulating lighting and exhibits suspended from the ceiling. There are the glass lifts, the children's café and, of course, the IMAX. The permanent exhibition featuring locomotives, jet planes and cars is so beautifully put together it is awe inspiring.

The Bethnal Green Museum of Childhood is much lower key, and it concentrates on interspersing its untouchable childhood artefacts with sand pits and other soft and malleable little installations. However, it still values the old-fashioned skills of looking and absorbing, displaying its hoard of

Above: Finding out how plants are pollinated at the Climbers and Creepers Zone at Kew Gardens.

treasures large and small for those tiny minds to study in detail. It trusts little children to be able to do this, and that is very important. And because it is not too big you can spend a short or long time there and always feel that it has been valuable.

The Dulwich Picture Gallery is an interesting mix of old and new. The gallery itself is Victorian. It has been refurbished, but is nonetheless a picture gallery in the old style. But the rooms are small, and exhibitions tend to be small-scale, so that if you are young the experience is not too overwhelming or exhausting. Linking the museum to the café is a very pretty cloister, and the café itself uses glass to feel accessible, very modern and airy. I have had very successful visits there with children who are not too stimulated by the gallery space to be distracted from enjoying and absorbing the pictures. The whole feel is unfussy and uncluttered.

The Guggenheim Bilbao, however, is at the other end of the scale. It is even more amazing than a Disney palace – like a vast shell from the sea shore magnified a million times, a cathedral for our 21st century of the unexpected, wild and beautiful. It is so exotic, so blatantly sensuous, so Spanish. It makes you want to run and explore, and also just stand and look up at the ceiling. And there are no machines, no handles to pull, no art presented as a fruit machine.

At Kew, nature enters the mix. And the idea of the interdependence of plants and animals, the built world and the garden around it is a very important one for young minds to grasp.

But there is another, equally important and not necessarily contradictory consideration – it needn't be a case of either/or. While the movement to welcome children has to be applauded, I can't help longing a little bit for the old style feeling of contemplation. Art is something that you experience when you are tranquil and receptive. It is very much an act of worship; the workings of a vast machine are as inspirational as an Egyptian cat. While I feel it is a really welcome advance that our children should enjoy our museums, I also think that to cultivate a receptive, quiet space in which to contemplate our culture and history has to be one of the keys not only to preserving the past, but to building something civilised for the future. In an age of fast travel, absurdly speedy communications, the gizmo, the constant hovering of an alternative surreal world of simulated virtual reality, we need to hold on to the human aspect of making art, showing it, and absorbing it, because that is how its spirit is passed on. Children can be trusted to quietly observe, even if it is only for a minute or two. I think often we fear we must stimulate them or they will lose interest. Balance is key.

The Pattern Pod, The Science Museum, London

Wilkinson Eyre Architects

Client: The Science Museum
Completion Date: June 2000

The Pod forms a small semi-enclosed space in the giant floor of the new wing at the museum. It is a small and manageable space, distinctive for its combination of dimness and intense lighting and the variety of simple but complex interactive exhibits on offer.

The Science Museum has always led the way when it comes to children's exhibits. From its opening in 1928, it established a hands-on push-button approach, showing working demonstrations of the inner mechanics of mysterious machines. In 1931 it opened the Children's Gallery where demonstrations of planets orbiting the sun, phones emitting a low frequency sound only discernible to children and dioramas of 3-D scenes were but a few of the attractions. In 1931 the first automatic doors were put on display, revealing the pressure pads that could be pressed to operate the same magic doors to the future we now take for granted. Practical wonder is the Science Museum's stock in trade.

With the building of the new Wellcome wing in 2000, attention was given to the first space for the very young, the Pattern Pod. It forms part of a huge triple-height black-floored space that houses the escalators to the IMAX 3-D cinema. In the basement below is the large indoor play area for older children known as the Launch Pad, (originally built in 1986 and revised in 2000). The Pattern Pod was devised by architects, exhibit designers and lighting experts in partnership with the Science Museum. It is egg-shaped, a low curved wall marking it off from the rest of the area, but preserving a sense of space and intimacy. There is no ceiling, it is open to the vast full height of the main space. There is a curved bench for the children and their carers, and various interactive exhibits for them to attach themselves to. These exhibits took three years to design, test and finish. A footprint exhibit mimics a young child's crawling pattern, another has a touch pad that produces coloured patterns on a screen. There is also another hut-like space, behind a curtain, marked off from the rest of the pod like a confessional, where coloured lights mimic the movement of the child as it dances or moves.

The whole pod is dynamically and dramatically lit, with pools of coloured light making patterns on the floor. Objects are either lit from above or within, in a conscious echoing of the feeling of the shafts of light that illuminate the underwater world. The overall ambience is remarkably dim, an effect both soothing and overpowering.

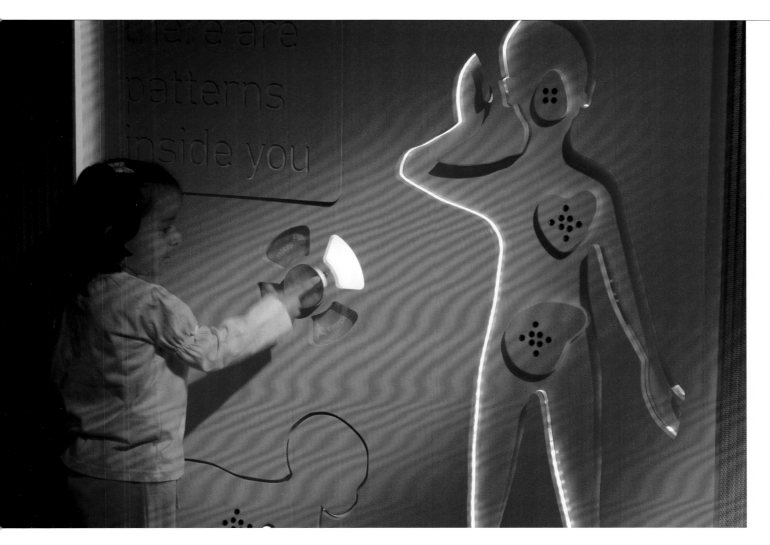

there are
patterns
inside you

Above: **The Pattern Pod, London.** Carefully designed, the interactive display panels both delight and inform. You can see how engaged this little girl is with this installation

The designers wanted to avoid primary colours, giant toys, soft materials, features often synonymous with indoor children's spaces. The emphasis is on discovery, of the senses and of the body's movement. 'If I press this, this will happen, if I stamp my feet on the pressure pad, that will happen.' Fractals – the ever-blooming replicating of a pattern or shape – are everywhere. There are costumes for dressing up, and of course, a water feature.

Educators and designers argue that the interactive environment is empowering for the child. It could also be seen as the inevitable precursor to the video game and the virtual experience, through encouraging in its patterns of mimicry, a certain narcissism. I can't help but feel that a sand pit and a paddling pool, with natural light, or a tub of glue and some coloured shapes might do just as well. Because for all the theory about freedom and self-expression the experience and its results – though beautiful – are inherently prescribed.

Left: **The Pattern Pod, London.** Children making
sense of puzzle patterns together

Dulwich Picture Gallery, London

Rick Mather

Client: Dulwich Picture Gallery
Completion Date: 2000

The picture gallery captures the past for small children and with its layout of modern cloister, additional rooms and excellent café, makes a little world that feels enlightened and calm. A perfect size for children without being miniaturised or scaled down.

England's oldest purpose-built gallery was opened in 1811 and is widely regarded as an architecturally significant building. By the end of the 20th century, however, it was in such a state of disrepair and provided so few facilities that it not only received dwindling visitor numbers, but it was also proving inadequate to house and conserve its collection of old masters.

The refurbishment has repaired the main building, closing off some windows to add more hanging space, and replacing damaging fluorescent lighting with carefully controlled natural light. Further office space and picture storage have been added.

The additional buildings – cafeteria, multi-purpose room for lectures and temporary exhibitions, washrooms and education centre – are connected to the main gallery via a cloister. It is such a simple, perfect idea. A cloister immediately provides the sense of an enclosed, private world of knowledge, closely connected to the past. But it is also light and practical, giving the gallery a feeling of being an accessible jewel in the crown. It also brings the garden into harmony with the buildings. Children love a cloister, because they like a feeling of secrecy. Also it provides a path to follow and is great for running along. And the whole design does not fight with the gallery, but enhances it beautifully. A modern London quadrangle to sit equally with those of Oxford, Paris or Rome.

Because the main gallery is so small it's ideal for a children's outing. Examine a few pictures in detail, and off to the café. The cloister is glazed and the windows slide back in good weather. It also has rooflights to provide an even greater sense of light. The café is also glazed on two sides, so you can sit and look back at the gallery and garden and still feel part of the experience you have just enjoyed. In summer, its windows slide back too, allowing the space to spill out on to the terrace. It is a comfortable, small, civilised size, and there is table service, which is just so much nicer than queuing when you are with little children.

This gallery has been described as both London's most perfect art gallery and the most beautiful small gallery in the world. I would agree.

Opposite: **Dulwich Picture Gallery, London.**
Summer on the café terrace - just a hop, skip and a jump from the gallery

Below: **Dulwich Picture Gallery, London.** A view of the cloister and café from the gallery. The building sits lightly in its natural surroundings

Above: Dulwich Picture Gallery, London.
Inside the gallery the space is warm and gently
lit. The size of the gallery is perfect for children
– no vast echoing halls and long corridors here

Guggenheim Museum, Bilbao, Spain

Gehry Partners

Client: Solomon R. Guggenheim Foundation
Completion Date: 1997

Striking, surprising and enticing, you can be safe to assume that your child will never have seen anything like it. The building echoes so many forms in nature, sculpture and architecture, and yet is utterly unique.

The Guggenheim Bilbao may not at first seem like a children's building, but it has got the works: adventure, mystery, excitement, style and true glamour. If you want to take small children somewhere that will truly stretch their imaginations and their idea of what a building can be, what space and light and colour are, it has to be your number one destination. It is truly wondrous. It is also beautifully situated on the banks of the River Nervion at the edge of a piazza that also houses the Museo de Bellas Artes, the university, and the old town hall.

The main entrance to the museum is through a large central atrium, where curvilinear bridges, glass elevators and stair towers connect the exhibition galleries concentrically on three levels. This central atrium is built on an unprecedented scale, rising to a height of more than 50 meters above the river. Special events and installations are held in this main space. Here, the under fives can crane their little necks at the sculptural roof rising above the atrium and flooding it with light through glazed openings in much the same way as stained glass windows in a cathedral or the high windows in the domes of mosques. So it is a stimulating place to make the connection between the great buildings of the past and those of the present and future. This is a temple to art and the imagination, and building as a monument to nature.

All these peculiar asymmetrical spaces are so enticing they can make you feel giddy. While a visit to the museum may not last long, it is full of surprise, and prompts questions along with all the oohs and aahs of admiration. And there are so many textures and colours to absorb, the main three being Spanish limestone, titanium and glass. Throughout, the sculpture of this exciting building offers magnificent views of the river and city.

It's just a joy to behold. A must for the under fives.

Above: Guggenheim Museum, Bilbao. Imagine being very small and seeing this at the end of the road, something so gleaming, colossal, other-worldly, yet benign

Above: Guggenheim Museum, Bilbao. This suspended walkway gives a child an interior climbing frame with a view of a giant, and somewhat battered, shuttlecock and textured stone slabs. The sense of sculptured space is extraordinary

Right: Guggenheim Museum, Bilbao. If this were a film set this would be called the money shot. Amazingly, it is real: a cross between a cathedral dome, a sculpture and an iceberg – dizzying and awe-inspiring

Above: Climbers and Creepers Zone, Kew.
The generous space can accommodate many
different installations

On the arches: I'm a plant – you're only animals: you need me for food!   Watch out!   I'm thorny!

Above: Climbers and Creepers Zone, Kew.
Children experiencing the Bramble Tangle

Left: Climbers and Creepers Zone, Kew. This little child examines a Venus flytrap. There's also an installation close by where you can trigger the flytrap by throwing sticky pretend bugs in it

Above Climbers and Creepers Zone, Kew. A magnificent wooden snail stands in front of the brambles.

Opposite: Climbers and Creepers Zone, Kew.
Learning through play: children explore the field mouse's Hideaway Home

Roald Dahl Children's Gallery,
Aylesbury

Bremner & Orr Design Consultants

Client: Buckinghamshire County Museum
Completion Date: 1996

It is the hands-on objects rather than the spaces in this gallery that create an all-encompassing fantasy for children. Pieces, such as James's Giant Peach, engage them physically, triggering them to imagine themselves into Roald Dahl's stories. A very immediate way for young children to first encounter Dahl, it makes them curious to read on.

Quentin Blake, who illustrated Dahl's books, describes this gallery as like walking into a giant pop-up book of his own work. Housed in an eighteenth-century coach-house that is part of the Buckinghaumshire County Museum, the main focus of the gallery is the installations rather than the space itself. David Erskine, Exhibitions Manager at the Museum, describes it as 'one of a new breed of hybrids, a cross between a science centre and a museum'. He goes on to say: 'The Gallery has learnt much from science centres and some popular exhibits have been absorbed – the frozen shadows, bendy mirrors, optical illusions and videochromakey, for example. But instead of standing alone, as they do in many science centres, they are incorporated into the "Dahlesque" themes and the overall environment.'

The museum's intimacy (it has a capacity of only 85) and its unique hands-on exhibits enable it to create an all-encompassing world for children: there are large set pieces – such as James's Giant Peach, Fantastic Mr Fox's tunnel and the Twit's upside-down room – that enable visitors to create the illusion that they are the characters in Dahl's stories. For children familiar with Dahl, it is like visiting the books, having them animated around them. For those not already Dahl readers, each interactive experience is complete in itself.

The Discovery Gallery on the ground floor features James's Giant Peach and Fantastic Mr Fox's tunnel. At the end of the gallery, Matilda's Library is entered through an enormous book which houses audio points as well as books. Access to the first-floor Imagination Gallery is by the Great Glass Elevator, as featured in Charlie and the Chocolate Factory. In the upstairs gallery, children can discover the Twits' Upside-Down Room and an extraordinary object 'zoo'. There is also the Big Friendly Giant and George's Grandma among other characters.

The business of translating so specific an imaginary world into tangible reality is a tricky one. Certainly the pleasure of touching, jumping and exploring are entirely different to those journeys of the imagination, which are in the books. They provide an additional dimension or media in which to experience the Dahl stories.

Above: **Roald Dahl Children's Gallery, Aylesbury.**
In the ground-floor Discovery Gallery, large scale installations of James's Giant Peach and Fantastic Mr Fox's tunnel intersect with quentin Blake's much-loved illustrations

This museum is not the only museums dedicated to the author – the Roald Dahl Museum and Story Centre is also planned in Buckinghamshire, for Dahl's home village of Great Missenden (see pp 112-113). This translation of children's literature into a physical experience does for Roald Dahl what Disney did for the Brothers Grimm – it elucidates, communicates, popularises and, of course, definitely transforms.

Above: Roald Dahl Children's Gallery, Aylesbury.
Children await the Great Glass Elevator in the foyer,
just off the main ground-floor gallery

Below: **Roald Dahl Children's Gallery, Aylesbury.**
Upstairs in the Imagination Gallery is the Twits'
Upside-Down Room and a wall in which objects are
hidden. The intimacy of the space is emphasised
by the exposure of the rafters of the coach-house
that accommodates the gallery

Roald Dahl Museum and Story Centre, Great Missenden, Bucks

Bremner & Orr Design Consultants
Hawkins Brown Architects

Client: Roald Dahl Museum and Story Centre
Completion Date: summer 2005

The man behind the stories becomes as vivid as the characters in them in this new museum devoted to Roald Dahl. The experience of visiting a place where an author has lived, and which is decorated throughout by his characters (whether the Big Friendly Giant or a crocodile), provides a unique opportunity for young children to be introduced to the idea of storytelling.

Whereas the Roald Dahl Gallery in Aylesbury is devised around the characters to be found in Roald Dahl's books, this space revolves around the author himself. Due to be opened in June 2005, it is to be located in a coach-house in Great Missenden, the Buckinghamshire village where Roald Dahl (1916-1990) lived and wrote many of his stories. Dahl's writing hut will be recreated, providing a sense of the man himself. As well as housing his archive, there is also a Story Centre, inspired by Dahl's love of storytelling that will provide many opportunities for young children to interact with various displays.

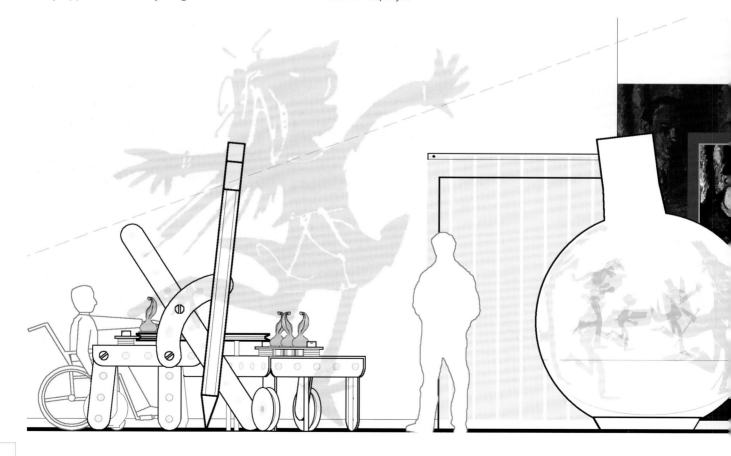

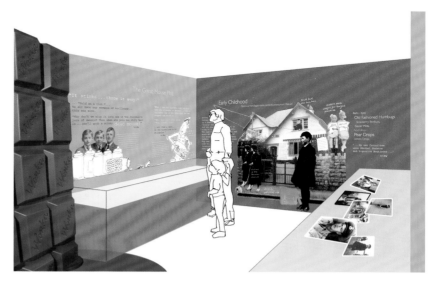

Right: Roald Dahl Museum and Story Centre, Great Missenden. New caption needed here. New caption needed here. New caption needed here

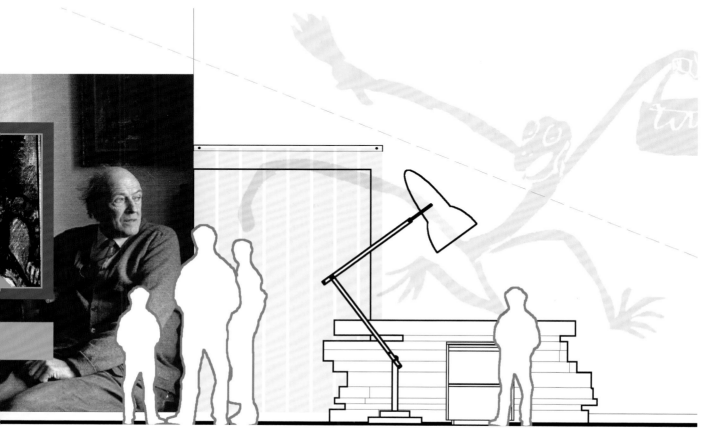

Discover Children's Centre, Stratford, London

Exhibition and Interior Designers: Bremner & Orr Design Consultants
Dannatt Johnson Architects

Client: Discover
Completion Date: 2003

Discover is called a story-building exhibition space. It attempts to recreate the abstract building blocks of stories as real structures or hyper-real experiences. So the age-old literary themes of escape, danger, flight and transformation are placed before the child in the form of installations and through them, physical play becomes imaginative play.

This exhibition space is a unique invention designed to serve the community of Stratford in East London, an area where there are over a hundred languages spoken. Developed over years of consultation with educationalists, schools and designers, it aims to stimulate the imaginations of both young children and their carers to invent and share stories. It is seen as very important to involve adults as well as children in the experience so that their relationship can be enhanced through imaginative play. Very shy or withdrawn children, or those with a variety of difficulties, can be helped in this way.

How it works is that the exhibition space houses a variety of quite complex installations. Each built installation has a guide or story-builder on hand to help each child begin to imagine a story. So there is the 'Do you Dare?' exhibition where a simulated stream, complete with the submerged backs of magical creatures, can be crossed via a wobbly bridge. There is a passage leading to a secret cave. From these props a story can be born. The same is true for the 'Giant's Feet' installation and the 'Lollipopter'. Others are more surreal, providing the full-on virtual experience. You can be inside a magic parcel, or in the 'Flying Pages' blue-screen 'shell' . . . feel what it is like to disappear down a drain and fly over the rooftops of Stratford.

The designers intend the children to feel completely immersed in the space, so aimed for a colour saturation of red, silver, gold and blue and a very theatrical use of light. It is certainly an overwhelming sensory experience, employing a wide range of techniques to stimulate little children. How they respond is a matter for their personalities and the way they are guided. It could well be that something simpler could do the trick just as well, but what is certain is that this is a Centre dedicated to children in a place where one is very much needed. There is also a story garden outside to be used in good weather.

Below: **Discover Children's Centre, London.** The use of colour and dramatic lighting is powerful in the entrance space, while a ticket desk on wheels signals how objects will be used in a transformative way

Left: Discover Children's Centre, London. In the Do You Dare galllery, children can cross the wobbly wooden bridge – which is also suitable for wheelchairs – and explore the enclosures beyond, each containing an unexpected surprise

Below: Discover Children's Centre, London. The Lollipopter installation can stand for anything with a fuselage: a helicopter, a plane or a boat. Children can pretend to buy travel tickets to get on board

Above **Discover Children's Centre, London.** In the Blue Screen room children are given the virtual experience of seeing themselves shooting down a drain and flying over Stratford, as their figures are blended with a backdrop of a pre-recorded video

Right: **Discover Children's Centre, London.** A mirror on the opposite wall shows the children what they would look like if these were their feet. Through windows, there are also legs disappearing into infinity (or the floors above) painted on a lightwell beyond

Discovery Center, The American Museum of Natural History, New York

CR Studio Architects PC

Client: The American Museum of Natural History, Education Department
Completion Date: June 2001

The architects have knitted together disparate spaces, aiming to create a new, carefully choreographed and intimate experience within the larger complex of the museum.

The Discovery Center was created to give children an introduction to the museum. It's an interactive educational space representing all major sciences, from anthropology to astrophysics. It is made of up three rooms: a circular room with 20 foot ceilings which forms the basis of one of the original 19th-century turrets, another long narrow rectangle of a space with the same height ceiling, and a mezzanine that connects the main staircase and the hall next to it. The main level is the place for children from three to ten while the mezzanine caters for ten and older, because it incorporates more advanced technological tools.

Very strikingly and making its point, the turret space houses the baobab tree, described by the architects as an icon of biodiversity. It's a wonderfully immediate way of telling at least one of the stories of the museum. The long rectangular space holds a Northwest Native American Indian totem pole, another icon of a different if equally impressive kind.

In designing the space, the architects uncovered and refurbished existing windows to create a learning environment that incorporates changing daylight. Colour is used boldly. The three different spaces go from hot to warm to cool through a combination of colour changes, the screening of daylight, and materials selection. A material's colour or texture is used to enhance a particular exhibit or lend a tone to the space: paleontology is hot in colour whereas astrophysics is cool. This distinction is very important for children, who can become accustomed to bleached spaces, and it helps make the exhibits more vibrant and alive.

A microcosm of the museum, the Discovery Center is a great starting point for children in their appreciation and understanding of science and nature.

Above: Discovery Center, New York. The entrance to the Center, green and fresh, and clearly delineated from the rest of the Museum

Opposite: Discovery Center, New York. The lively colours echo those of the totem pole, bringing the past into the environment of the present

Above: Discovery Center, New York. The lack of clutter in this study area allows the true and simple exhibits their full impact

Right: Discovery Center, New York. Careful attention is given to height in displaying and storing objects

Above: Discovery Center, New York. The tree can be appreciated from different angles and levels, or children can sit and talk about their impressions under its branches

PLAY

Above: One of the several dedicated play areas at the Great Ormond Street Hospital in London that have helped to transform a child's experience of a hospital visit.

one's turn on the slide – but there's nothing wrong with that. And then, once they've worked up an appetite, you can proceed directly to the café without passing 'Go'.

At the Grudzien Residence in Hong Kong, small play spaces have been devised alongside the adult spaces. The little cave space under the stairs is ideal for camping, and then the graffiti walls in the children's bedrooms are perfect for self-expression without the neatness demanded by books. When I was young, we had a dedicated wall in our playroom that we divided into squares of about 12 inches. In each square we painted a different picture, and children and grown-ups who came to the house were always invited to paint a square if they wanted. This was tremendous fun and a way of giving some freedom to children and a feeling of value for their work.

The Hotel Tresanton playroom is a gorgeously simple space: ice cream colours, a practical and stylish mosaic floor, French windows, little wipeable but trendy tables and chairs, and a screen for film and video time. The whole design echoes the seashore in its light and simplicity.

The little tree house in North London may not be the magnificent timber structure that so many of today's treehouses are, but it is absolutely magical in its gossamer delicacy, its sense of mystery and privacy. It makes me want to be under five again, just to have a chance to climb into it!

St Mary's Church Hall in Wimbledon is another blank slate. There is the low slice of window which shows the flowerbed on one side, and the glass wall to the garden on the other. The rest is a rectangle, to do whatever you jolly well like in.

Selfridges Kids in London is an oddity. I've included it as a playspace because it has so much to stimulate a tiny brain that, although it's really a shop, shopping seems almost secondary. The illuminated ceiling, the royal blue carpet, the strange white installations – it's rather like a magical mystery tour. The only difficulty is scraping children off the floor and getting them to leave.

The little playhouses – one thatched, the other shingle roofed – conform to the quintessential ideal of the old-fashioned playhouse. Here they represent the 19th-century dream Beatrix Potter bequeathed to us of dainty domesticated creatures imitating adult life in miniature houses. Although this may not be especially fashionable now, it gets most children's votes. They love anything tiny – scale is a big preoccupation for small children – and there is plenty of furniture just perfect for their cooking, sweeping and cleaning games. It can't be pirates and fairies all of the time. Children love playing houses; it forms the solid fabric of their everyday lives.

I think all these spaces exhibit a real thoughtfulness about different aspects of children's play, and they are conceived with refreshing simplicity.

Below: As bright and shiny as any conventional toy shop, Future Systems' toy department for Selfridges in London tempts play and interaction with all the different items on the shelves.

Blue Kangaroo, King's Road, London

Penny Morris and Tony Hagdrup

Client: Blue Kangaroo
Completion Date: September 2003

A winning combination of restaurant and play space, its large-scale internal playframe and child friendly interior invite younger visitors to eat up and then join in the fun; unobtrusive CCTV allows adults to relax and still keep an eye on things.

Blue Kangaroo restaurant and playspace is the brainchild of Tony Hagdrup and his friend Adam Duthie. As parents of young children they were tired of travelling to out of town warehouse conversions and freezing to death holding Styrofoam cups of coffee while their children played on the vast padded playframes that have become so popular for the very young. Their question was,

Below: **Blue Kangaroo, London.** The upstairs dining room includes a closed-circuit TV screen, so that parents can keep an eye on their children in the play area

Above: **Blue Kangaroo, London.** Down the slide to happiness in the basement playframe

why shouldn't the whole experience of indoor play be more civilised, and provide a happy space for both child and parent?

The answer, they felt, was to combine a good lunch – or cup of tea or coffee – in a centrally located building on a smaller, more human scale, with the freedom for children to let off steam and play in an open frame.

Blue Kangaroo is designed on two floors. The ground floor houses a brasserie, light and airy and simply furnished with wooden chairs and leather banquettes. Downstairs is the café, a small soft area for babies, and the bright, primary coloured playframe, which has been sunk into both floors, though it is only accessible from below. Once their children have passed the precarious toddler stage, it is theoretically possible for adults to eat lunch while their children play downstairs unsupervised, because there is close circuit TV beaming up images of what is going on below.

If all that seems a bit Big Brother, the whole family can eat upstairs in the well laid out spacious dining room where the diversion provided by two train sets guarantees a fairly trouble-free lunch before repairing below. Equally, parents can eat down in the cafe while they keep an eye on their children. There are magazines laid out on all the tables, thoughtful cubbyholes for shoes, and easy access in two places to the climbing frame for both children and adults. The playframe's primary colours are offset with white paint in the café and friendly groups of pale tables and chairs. The whole premises are security-locked from the inside.

While it is true that the children are mostly in a state of wild and noisy excitement, and the adults still mostly on guard, the atmosphere is happy. Combining a grown-up menu and comforts with a child's dream come true certainly highlights the way adults' and children's experiences and needs are now seen as distinct and separate. Instead of a nice lunch together in a situation where children are expected to behave as adults, rehearsing the roles they will one day assume, followed by a trip to park, museum or zoo, here they can get down from the table and wander off downstairs to play. It is a cleverly customised environment that shows how manners and mores are changing; and the locked door to the world outside illustrates even more how play has been forced off the streets and even away from parks, and into a more controlled situation.

This giant, cosy, small-scale playpen for adults and children is proving a winning combination.

Above: Blue Kangaroo, London. A well equipped
soft playframe for under threes is located off to one
side on the ground floor

Right: **Blue Kangaroo, London.** Children enjoy crayons with their milkshakes

Right: **Blue Kangaroo, London.** Inside the larger playframe – sociable and fun

Grudzien Residence, Hong Kong

Denise Ho Architects

Client: Mr Julian and Mrs Pam Grudzien
Completion Date: December 2003

This apartment's thoughtful design shows how a small space can be adapted for two children and parents who work at home – with areas designed for specific uses, and plenty of storage.

Within a relatively small apartment, Denise Ho Architects have designed a space for the whole family, where children and adults can be together and still feel separate: somewhere safe, practical and very imaginative.

Space constraints have demanded careful thought – the design is informed by the reality of a small apartment catering for a growing family. But what they have created feels so generous and light, it's a testament to their effort and careful planning.

The main space incorporates a play area for the children – aged one and a half and three – as well as a work station for their father. This might seem doomed as a combination, but it works. Sliding doors separate the spaces.

There is also a beautiful spacious open shelving unit that overlays the stairs, with children's storage at the lower levels, and the parents' books, CDs and ornaments above. Under the stairs is a tiny den, a small private space for the children.

The wall between the children's bedrooms has been knocked down, and curtains lead from each child's room into a walk-in closet between the bedrooms – fun for hide and seek, but also practical. There is minimal furniture in their rooms – just a bed and a deck, leaving as much room for play as possible. Drawers and hangars are at low level to provide easy access for the children. The closet also has a sea view which the children can glimpse by clambering on top of the little drawers of their storage unit. There are also plenty of wooden storage boxes and little stools for the children. Their parents can sit on the floor to read them a story.

Each child has a whole wall in their bedroom known as the 'graffiti wall'. It is a large piece of board fixed to the wall and rendered to give a smooth surface that can receive any media of colour, acrylic paint, pastels, even coloured pencils. Paintings can be done and then painted over, so that the wall is an ongoing work and play in progress for the children.

Furniture is fastened to the floor. Light switches are placed very low down. In the living room, the built-in television is mounted so as to be at a comfortable level for the children when they sit down. The master bedroom is almost cleared of furniture so that the children can play close to their parents on lazy mornings. The heavily carpeted staircase is also intended for the children to use as a play area/climbing frame, although, of course, there is a stair gate at the top.

It is really interesting to see how many activities have been catered for in this small space, so devoid of clutter. There is tremendous scope for these young children to work, sleep, play and be with their parents – something often neglected in designing for children. The space is rigorously planned, and the architects have never forgotten the three s's: storage, storage, storage.

Below: Grudzien Residence, Hong Kong. The shelf unit screening the staircase is clean and elegant, and makes the space look bigger

Above: Grudzien Residence, Hong Kong.
Overview of the main living spaces, with the work
station and study at the far end of the room

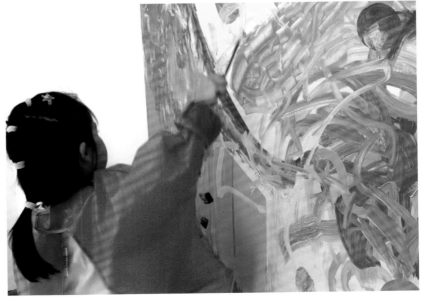

Right: **Grudzien Residence, Hong Kong.** The curtains dividing the children's bedrooms conceal the closet space between them

Opposite and left: **Grudzien Residence, Hong Kong.** Both children's bedrooms include large graffiti walls in the form of large boards that can be painted over or replaced

Hotel Tresanton, St Mawes, Cornwall

Olga Polizzi

Client: Olga Polizzi, Tresanton Hotel
Completion Date: 2003

The children's building at this seaside hotel follows the classic paradigm of ice cream colours and restful space allowing for the play of light. It's also modern, practical and designed for painting, play or watching a film.

This is the most gentle and restful of all the children's interiors featured here, partly because of the seaside light and partly because of the design's simplicity.

The floor is mosaic – very practical – but also fun for children to trace the words and their patterns. And the black and cream is bold without being jarring. The walls are a gentle cream colour. The garden, with its friendly playhouse, is always visible through the French windows. The little chairs are the classic Modernist design in 1950s' pastels, the trestle tables are low, the shelves accessible.

You can't help thinking that if you were staying in this wonderful hotel you would feel completely relaxed about sending your children off to play and eat and watch movies in this building. It doesn't have that uninviting air of a spare space converted quickly and kitted out on the cheap to put the children in while the adults relax. Nothing screams 'children's space' at you. There are no powerful colours, no images, figurative or abstract encroaching on little brains, no logos, no cartoon characters, no bright lights, no gadgets, no themed experience. It is all about being in a pleasant, almost enlightenment atmosphere with other children and carers, and that's it. Like a detox for the young mind.

What is also remarkable is that the rooms are very like the adult spaces in the hotel. They too rely on light, views of the sea, natural materials and neutral colours. They too allow the outside to come into the rooms and nothing in the rooms to impose itself, but everything is orderly, well proportioned and beautiful.

There is also a sense of a nurturing femininity in the spaces. They are neither bland nor obstinately white and blank like so many modern designs. Nor are they irritatingly dull. It is all about balance. And here, children, instead of being treated as sensation addicts, are given the peace and quiet that their parents continually crave.

A dream come true.

Above: **Hotel Tresanton, St Mawes.** Buckets and spades, pretty French window, practical and unusual floor – like the seaside, only better

Above: **Hotel Tresanton, St Mawes.** The view
of the garden and playhouse

Right: **Hotel Tresanton, St Mawes.** The
children's room is calm and restful, but is well
supplied with activities to engage children even
on the wettest day

Twenty-first Century Treehouse, London

Stephen Gage

Client: Isobel Gage
Completion Date: 2002

This is not your average treehouse, echoing a log cabin or a rustic historical idyll. Its material and design make it both new and as timelessly organic as a butterfly wing.

A treehouse is a place of great delight for a child.

To begin with there is the feeling of danger and slight rebellion about leaving the house, the domesticated space, behind. After that there is the secrecy: once you are in a treehouse you are practically invisible. Then there is the feeling of height, being suspended between earth and sky, but utterly still, not flying. That gives a certain power. And then there is the feeling of the age, solidity and beauty of the tree that provides the architecture for the little, balanced, precarious space. Being in a treehouse is like being in a shipwreck, or on a treasure hunt, or sleeping in the arms of the moon; it's like running away, building your own camp, living to your own time.

A treehouse is serene, yet magical and exciting. A treehouse that a child could imagine building for itself – and one without decoration or design or paint or furniture – is the best. If you want to carry up paints and paper or a book or a sleeping bag or a friend, you can; but it's just as much fun to be quite alone looking at the tree tops and the sky. The treehouse makes solitude happy, a place of exploration, not boredom and confinement.

There are many treehouses to choose from. You can have large wooden houses with balconies and ladders and even ones with more than one storey – a sort of millionaire's treehouse. But in my opinion, the best are the smallest and simplest.

The twenty-first century treehouse is by far the weirdest treehouse ever. It is like the bottom of a boat surrounded by a synthetic cone, reminiscent of a butterfly's wing, with no ceiling. It is insubstantial, diaphanous, highly theatrical. Secret. It reinvents the hearty, hoary timber-hewn Robinson Crusoe fantasy into a wild and feminine transformative fairy space.

Right: **Twenty-first Century Treehouse, London.**
Once up the twenty-first century ladder, you close the twenty-first century trapdoor and float away on your sky punt

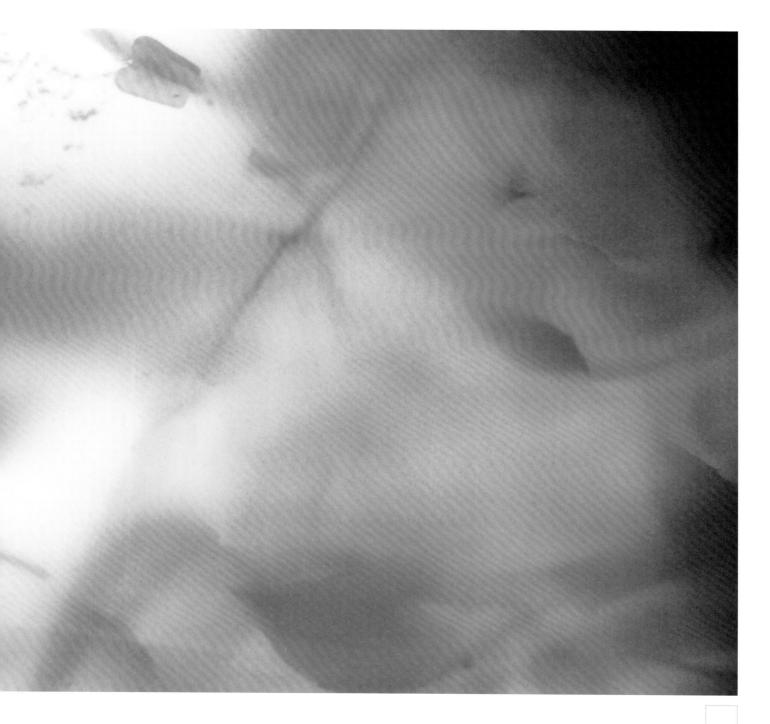

Below: **Twenty-first Century Treehouse, London.**
The way the light and leaves show through the translucent plastic makes for a magical experience and the fairy makes it the more so

Above: Twenty-first Century Treehouse, London.
From below the treehouse looks like a giant Moses
basket suspended in the trees

Above: **Twenty-first Century Treehouse, London.**
Pride

Above: **Twenty-first Century Treehouse, London.**
Up the stairs and through the trapdoor into a world
of one's own making

Above: **St Mary's Garden Hall, London.** The view from the garden into the hall

Right: **St Mary's Garden Hall, London.** A dry-stone wall in Wimbledon adds rustic charm and simplicity, and makes the building look part of its surroundings – an addition rather than an imposition

Selfridges Kids, Oxford Street, London

Future Systems
Client: Selfridges
Completion Date: 2001

Combining fun palace and play space, the lighting and design evoke the ambience of the 1960s for adults while children are captivated by the Disneylike touches. The ultimate shopping experience for parent and child.

Strange though it may have seemed even a decade ago to consider children as consumers quite as much as we now do, and ambivalent as we may feel about it, it is an undeniable fact. If parents shop for fun, so do children. Often it is a way of imagining things together, picking objects up, trying them on for size. It is no longer just about necessity. The experience is the thing. To avoid the inevitable boredom – the supermarket shopping syndrome of dragging kids around the shops – a place has to be really appealing and fun. Tangible, visual fun. And you can't get much more fun than this children's shopping world at Selfridges, London.

Above and opposite: **Selfridges Kids, London.**
The pods stand out like boulders in a man-made river and, up above, an impossible illuminated sky

Marked off from the main shop floor by a double red ribbon line at foot and head height that provides a boundary to imitate the curves of man-made hills or waves in gleaming frozen white, the whole design is immensely tactile. Hanging spaces for clothes are made out of white asymmetrical pods suspended from the ceiling on extra narrow wires, dangling feet away from the floor. Like hammocks, a child must want to climb into them. A collection of what looks like a cross between a boxing punch bag and a bean bag dangles down. Inside there are a selection of shoes. Little shallow scooped out trays are filled with knick-knacks just asking for little hands to bury themselves in them and pull out the perfect goody.

The carpet is a kind of Snow White royal blue, a peculiar, unnatural, gaudy and gorgeous colour. But the ceiling is the best part. It looks like the underside of a space ship, or a night sky canopy with impossibly large and swollen stars. Bright white light beams down creating a variety of patterns and effects.

For the grown-ups, there is something very knowing and '60s' Retro about the design, somewhere between the Sleeper set and the Avengers. To children it must seem just brand spanking new.

Above: **Selfridges Kids, London.** The shoe
display, with seating and display stands matching
the curvilinear forms of the clothes pods

Above: Selfridges Kids, London. An irresistible way to showcase a display of teddy bears and other soft toys

Left: Selfridges Kids, London. The larger pods serve many purposes – breaking down the space, providing seating and acting as a display stand, here for a dramatic three-dimensional race track

Left: Selfridges Kids, London. Screened by display pods, a quiet place to rest, or sit and look at books

Right: Selfridges Kids, London. With displays as colourful as these, it is so tempting to scoop up an armful of toys

Above: **Selfridges Kids, London.** The pods are arranged around the space like vast stepping stones in water, with delicate stalactites dangling above them

Children's Playhouses, Crediton, Devon

The Children's Cottage Company

Client: Private
Completion Date: 2003

These little houses are the quintessential old-fashioned English child's play houses with an attention to detail in design and construction that shows dedication and care.

Both these cottages were shown at the Chelsea Flower Show, 2003, with furniture provided by Dragons of Walton Street.

One little cottage has a thatched roof, the other has shingle. One little cottage has a garden, the other has none. One has fairies as a theme, the other Peter Rabbit. But one thing is for certain, they are the absolute ideal of Englishness – little Tardises of the history of British upper-class and bourgeois childhoods, profoundly in the tradition of the Englishman's folly. They belong to the vernacular of childhood tamed, miniaturised, and domesticated – for all the superficial wildness of the animals and fairies. They are the kind of thing that would make a Modernist architect flinch – but children love them and ordinary adults cannot fail to be charmed.

The workmanship is superb. The thatch on the thatched cottage is trimmed to within an inch of its life, the porch beautifully constructed and painted. It looks solid and permanent, which completes the illusion of it belonging to another, tiny and perfect world.

Play in these cottages relies on the fun of the distorted miniature scale, and imitating grown-up life. But it's also very much connected to that feeling of ownership and privacy which children long for. Although it might be about playing at being grown up, the rules of the game are the children's.

Although the cottages appear perfect in their tiny tidy symmetry, there is something a little eerie about the way the proportions are skewed. The trim on the overhang of the porch is exaggerated and the furniture is also big for the spaces. While this might appear surreal to adults, it probably feels perfectly natural to children, who are used to seeing things as oversized. But if you wanted to furnish the interiors more minimally, that's possible too.

The feeling of a stage set for children to fill with imaginary industry – in the house as well as the garden – is overpowering. It's up to the children whether to subvert this expectation – like Peter Pan – or sit and sew on the porch like Wendy.

Above: **Children's Playhouse.** The only thing that beats one playhouse is two playhouses together

Opposite: **Children's Playhouse.** You are never too young to start gardening. The range of finishes and accessories is nearly limitless

Left: Children's Playhouse. Every detail has been considered – inside and out

Below: Children's Playhouse. The inside of Peter Rabbit's cottage. Again there is a play on scale, with a giant Peter Rabbit and a small grandfather clock.

Right: **Children's Playhouse.** A triumph of opulence, stuffed with furniture, including the all-important crib for playing baby games

Above: **Children's Playhouse.** Inside, the fairy cottage is jam packed with all things homey – curtains, cushions and, of course, the all important stove. It is a little like Alice in Wonderland for these over fives but perfect for younger children. Note, too, the ladder and the clock

Left: **Children's Playhouse.** The perfect thatched cottage. All it needs are the roses around the door

WATER

The first nine months of our lives are spent in water and that must explain the happiness so many of us feel when we return to it. Children and grown-ups instinctively float, turn, curl and curve their bodies to imitate the seahorse shapes of the baby in the womb. Surprisingly, newborns seem averse to water, it's as if being born is such a shock they have to give their all to accommodate themselves to dry land and don't want to be reminded and confused. They hate water splashed or trickled on their heads, and take a good few months before they will be happy immersed in a swimming pool. Bath a baby once it's no longer new, and they often go into an almost trance like state, suspended in their mother's arms, returning to their first element with ease. Equally, they can shriek, protest, flail their limbs around and turn red as boiled sweets. Changing elements is a transformation that is full of mystery, awe and lurking danger. Learning to swim can be as easy as a duck taking to water or a very tricky business. It is as if children have to relearn what they once knew: how to be relaxed in the water. Apprehension has the upper hand.

Water

Still, children are irresistibly drawn to water. I remember taking my niece to the seaside when she was about eight months old, my sister putting her down on the sand; like a turtle she started to shunt herself towards the gleaming water, pulling herself along by her arms. We laughed, she looked so comical and clumsy, so determined, but it was an extraordinary sight. Water for a baby or child can seem limitless, but she wasn't put off, longing for the infinite, the grandeur and excitement. When an adult stands on the beach they see to the horizon and can feel liberated. If you are of small child height you might not even see where sea meets sky. Wonderful and terrible.

Children are fascinated by the sheer size and majesty of the sea but even bath water can be unpredictable, let alone a swimming pool. But with growing confidence and encouragement and a little more time, there is also the tremendous fun of water games; of splashing and sliding, slipping and running on the grass and chasing under the sprinkler; of coolness on a hot day. A cherished memory of childhood for so many grown-ups.

And there are the hours on the beach with nets and buckets and spades, paddling in estuaries, making dams, castles with moats, or great smooth hills of sand decorated with shells. On the beach they can make and create. They can be busy, absorbed without everyday interruptions. And there is the mesmerising quality of the minute; a drop of water falling from the finger, all its sparkling beauty and separate glory lost instantly in the pool. The tide coming in can wreck a fortress, but while it exists, it is as large as a Hollywood set for that child, and it is their own.

The seashore provides contact with the infinite, and a subconscious sense of the age of the planet, the elements and of the millennia it has taken

Above: With its vast horizon, the sea provides an inkling of the great forces behind the natural world, but also offers easy chances to play.

Above: An interior like that of Shirokane Preschool in Tokyo designed by Atelier Suda Architects can capture the essence of this idyllic time paddling in the sea's shallows and bring it inside.

to forge that particular intersection between earth, sky and water. That timeless feeling is beyond words, and children respond to it keenly.

The sea hides the underwater world, swallows up flotsam only to spew it forth on some distant shore. Beneath the surface is another kingdom: of coral, flying fish, crabs, jellyfish, lobster, the enormous whale, the predatory shark, the great shoals moving along the sea bed like clouds across the sky. That sense of mystery appeals to the young imagination – nature untamed, the secret kingdom of giant octopuses, gentle dolphins and fish with the faces of angels and of clowns. They say space is the final frontier, but they have forgotten the sea.

There is also the soothing quality of water, the fountain, the stream. Fountains are put in public parks, ornamental pointers to the visitor that they are in a place of play, that they may leave their ordinary selves behind. In hospitals, fountains provide tranquillity, mesmerising the onlooker with the play and sounds of water in motion, a reminder to the child within of the far wider wilder waterfalls in the natural world – the curtain of water covering rocks, concealing secret caves. Pennies in the fountain have a profound appeal for children, evoking treasure lost and found, the world of pirates, of Never Never Land and Peter Pan.

In this chapter I have featured different aspects of water: from the sparkling indoor stream at the Shirokane Preschool – so unexpected, surprising and joyous – to the tiny wooden bath in the wet room at Babington House, where the subdued light induces a dreamlike sensation that makes the water almost everything for the senses. Then there is the traditional municipal swimming pool at Horsham. A simple design yet with tremendous generosity, it uses wood and natural light to banish the clinical chlorine feeling of generations of public pools. It even comes complete with water slide and palm trees.

At the London Aquarium, the underwater world is illuminated and revealed. Better than any cartoon, it's the real thing. This aquarium certainly has the wow factor. When I took my three-year-old son, I was so worried he would be intimidated by the size of the main tank and the sharks and the

Left: Fishing for tiddlers at the London Natural History Museum's outdoor pond combines pleasure with learning.

myriad fish. There are so many contrasts, not only in terms of scale, but also between the brightness of the tank and the darkness of the corridors. But he absolutely loved it. Stretched his arms out against the glass and embraced it. His curiosity and his surrender to the flooding of his senses were amazing. The aquarium also provides plenty of small tanks featuring tiny fish and amphibious creatures, with explanations of their habitat and way of life. It is so important for children to be shown how the world is made, the wonder of it – not only the spectacle of the shark but the minutiae of plankton, and how important each detail is to the planet's equilibrium. It is up to us to teach them to cherish and conserve.

The Deep develops the idea of the underwater world and its connection to the land, in part through its spectacular seafront site, and in part because it is not just a tourist attraction; it's a lifelong learning centre, place of business and a research centre run in connection with the University of Hull. It has gravitas and grandeur and also the air of a laboratory, something magnificent, a continuation of the 19th-century project in 21st-century terms. This rubs off on children – the seriousness and high-tech appeal.

Water refracts light, is malleable, beautiful, transforming, overwhelming. It is a source of joy and knowledge, and so inextricably connected to the early years.

Shirokane Preschool, Tokyo, Japan

Atelier Suda Architects

Client: Shirokane Preschool
Completion Date: February 2000

Architects love to talk about opening up interior space to the outside world. Here it has actually been achieved, using sliding doors to the exterior and flexible space inside. All this and a stream too.

This preschool sits in the middle of Tokyo, but its whole design is intended to connect children not with the urban fabric, but with nature. This is not done just by creating an interior that seems to flow into the playground outside or by providing views of water and trees, but by bringing the inside into the building, and treating the building itself as something as tangible and alive as a forest.

The architects renovated the original hut-like building by adding a wooden two-storey extension, reinforced with steel to add strength and lightness. Classrooms are open to both north and west.

The playground and the buildings are connected. Nothing is static. This encourages children to perceive space freely and be creative. The woodwork is designed as furniture. Floors can become steps or puddles. Walls can be used as hiding places or blackboards, columns and frames can be decorating stands or benches. The walls operate as doors, and doors slide open and shut to make spaces cosy or large. Yet there is nothing tricksy about the interior, it feels simple and playful.

There are no crowded corridors. The wash basins are sited in full view of the main space to make it easy to reach them. But the general space is never boring because it can change its shape.

And there is abundant simplicity in the whole design: the climbing frame which doubles as lockers, the wooden steps that slide in and out. There is metamorphosis everywhere.

And the best thing of all is the magical indoor stream. A man-made riverbed where the water supply can be turned on and off at will is truly wonderful, original, beautiful. Paddling in a babbling brook with your friends in the middle of a school morning – what could be more fun?

Above: Shirokane Preschool, Tokyo. In summer
this magical waterfall – or floating water, as the
architects call it – ingeniously transforms work space
into a stream for happy play. The water spout
gushes rainwater on a wet day

Above: Shirokane Preschool, Tokyo. The simple movable boxes are highly adaptable and can be used to create individual or tiered seating or, as here, extend the stage

Above: Shirokane Preschool, Tokyo. Natural light floods the main space from carefully arranged rooflights above and from the external playground

Opposite: Shirokane Preschool, Tokyo. Pebbles look like jewels in the river-bed, providing extra movement and delight

Above: Shirokane Preschool, Tokyo. The large
space is broken up with sliding wooden partitions to
create smaller soundproof rooms when closed. Low
height cubby holes and basins are easily accessible
– not tucked away down a corridor

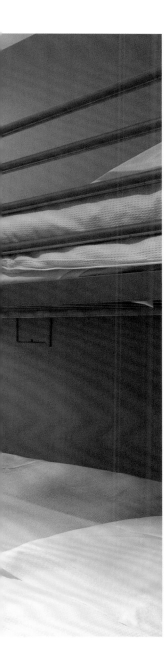

Left: Babington House, Somerset. Each of the five family rooms incorporates a child's bedroom, complete with bunk-beds, toys and a baby's changing table

Below: Babington House, Somerset. The wet rooms are calm and soothing. Adults and children alike can enjoy the large overhead shower, while the lid of a wooden seat at one end of the space can be removed to reveal a child-size bath

Pavilions in the Park, Horsham, Surrey

FaulknerBrowns
Client: Horsham District Council
Completion Date: 2002

Underneath its warm wooden barrel vaulting this pool has everything for the very young swimmer: gentle light, a slide to go down with parents and a separate pool well away from the action.

Pavilions in the Park is a vast sports complex on the edge of a public park close to Horsham town centre. Both adults and children visit regularly, and the key is to make this vast space somehow friendly to young children and as non-institutional as possible. The architects' aim was for it to be generous and welcoming to all ages.

The various spaces are cleverly connected using the friendly curves of large timber barrel vaulting for the roof. The look is vaguely reminiscent of a sailing boat – not a ceiling tile in sight. The curves are natural and rolling – a wooden sky canopy that provides a gentle acoustic for swimmers in the pool. (The wood is Forestry Stewardship Council accredited.) An impressive piece of design, the pools flow out from inside connecting the building with the park.

Inside, the building's hub is a winter garden, the planting providing another reminder of the parkland outside.

For young children in the pool there is the excitement of the curved water slide, designed to hold the infant and parent – it isn't a daunting, exposed slide. There is also a shallow pool, clearly defined for children, well away from the main pool. For fun there are the palm trees, and the natural light dapples the water and tiles so there isn't that feeling of public lavatory brightness and municipal harshness that was handed down to public spaces from the 1970s. This gentleness is enhanced by the natural colour of the wood, the louvres which provide ventilation, and the warmth of the locally made bricks used in the spine walls. It is so nice to escape from the total tyranny of glass used in so many show-off public buildings.

The building may not be landmark architecture like the Sydney Opera House, but it excites admiration all the same, and for a municipal swimming pool that is child friendly it scores ten out of ten. A gentle giant.

Above: **Pavilions in the Park, Surrey.** The pool flows from outside to inside

Above: **Pavilion in the Park, Surrey.** Sinuous water slide, wooden barrel vault and palm trees – all present and correct

Left: **Pavilions in the Park, Surrey.** Mother and child are entirely at home in this reflective curving water pool

London Aquarium, South Bank, London

RHWL Architects

Client: London Aquarium
Completion Date: 1997

This is spectacle on a grand scale for a young child, with low lighting and a whole new environment to absorb, complete with a myriad of fish and aquatic life. There is also the friendship pool, should you want to get acquainted with a stingray.

The London Aquarium is a very exciting place. It certainly doesn't feel like a museum, or even a zoo.

Queuing for tickets in its makeshift plasterboard lobby, there's no hint of the experience ahead. The air is full of children asking over and over, 'Where are the fish?' Then, once you go through the amusement park turnstiles and head down the steeply tilting corridor into darkness, an almost funfair atmosphere prevails. Little tanks house little jewel like fish. Seahorses. Coral. The scale is tiny, almost miniature. Small children have to be lifted to see inside.

At the centre of the serpentine design is the vast Atlantic Tank. This is huge and mysterious, viewed from two levels, from a height and from the base, the equivalent of the seabed. It is fabulous, dimly lit, mysterious, vast and full of sharks. But it does not present them in a threatening way, like extras in a James Bond film; rather the sharks drift in the water, relaxed, surrounded by smaller fish and plant life, at home.

There are no performing animals and no interactive exhibits. It is all about observing, and taking in what you see.

Very young children tend to lose themselves and just gaze at the element and the creatures in it, as though remembering the comforting waters of the womb. They are not frightened or shocked by the giant creatures, their dreamlike peculiarities. They take them for granted. The older children, who can grasp the complexities of scale, can be more taken aback, but also more curious, asking questions, wanting answers.

In the friendship pool, little ones can stretch their starfish hands out and touch the stingrays and fish and connect through more than just their eyes and consciousness with another element.

The labyrinth of the London Aquarium, its glamour, its foreignness, grandeur and low-lit beauty make it the perfect interior to stimulate the sense of wonder so characteristic of the very young child.

Below: **London Aquarium, South Bank.** Only a
pane of glass separates a young child from these
huge and fascinating predators

Above: **London Aquarium, South Bank.** The sheer scale of the main display inspires awe but not fear

Above: **London Aquarium, South Bank.** The friendship pool encourages little children to reach out without fear

Right: **London Aquarium, South Bank.** Up close and personal with a friendly ray

The Deep, Hull, Yorkshire

Terry Farrell & Partners

Client: Hull City Council with Millennium Commission
Completion Date: 2002

Lagoon of Light:
Exhibition concept – MET Studio
Exhibition designers – John Csaky and Associates
Young's Discovers' Corner – designed by The Deep's Chief Executive,
Colin Brown, and Curator, Dr David Gibson

The Deep presents the sea as enigmatic but understandable in a scientific way, so it's interesting to show a small child the enormity of what we believe we can harness and understand. And it's fun for all the family.

The Deep is an ambitious, exciting building and so innovative it has invented a name for itself – the Submarium. Looking out to sea like a cross between a vast ship, an iceberg and a shark, its architecture fuses its main themes: the link between the sea and the land, the submerged and the visible.

Built under the auspices of the Millennium Commission as part of the rejuvenation of Hull, it is the only building on the waterfront to offer commanding views – and to see and be seen in a confident visionary way.

Awe inspiring from the outside, inside it takes you on a journey from the top – the dawn of time – to the bottom – a fictional ocean research station studying the oceans of the past, present and future. As you walk past the huge undersea tanks, the impression is that you are going even deeper than you actually are; there's a sensation of compression. At the end – alarmingly or excitingly, depending on your point of view – you are shot up by means of a glass lift back to the third-floor viewing station, café and, of course, shop. So it is both a virtual and real experience, a magical mystery tour, but with a serious theme: you can learn about the sea here through your imagination, mind and senses.

If this whole enormous concept seems a bit much for a very young child, there are two specific points in the journey designed just for them. The Lagoon of Light is a nursery area for baby fish: bonnethead sharks, blue ribbontail rays, parrot fish, to name just a few. It is a clever idea to have the young identify with the young fish, and the walkway is just the right height for the little ones to observe independently and safely.

Then there is Young's Discovery Corner: a series of exciting touch pools housing Britain's rock pool creatures. It's like the British seaside holiday brought inside – from spider crabs, sea urchins, beadlet anenomes and spiny starfish to whelks. And there's nothing like being able to touch and feel protective over these non-threatening creatures to encourage children to feel a sense of guardianship over the natural world. All this and sharks, too.

Right: **The Deep, Hull.** The Lagoon of Light. The tank and walkway are designed to be just the right height for a child

Below: **The Deep, Hull.** This main space is so clean, like a laboratory opening on to the ocean. It doesn't look like a tank at all

Above: **The Deep, Hull.** Lagoon of Light – small
children admire a young bonnethead shark

Opposite: **The Deep, Hull.** It is such a delight to
be able to get this close to a sea creature

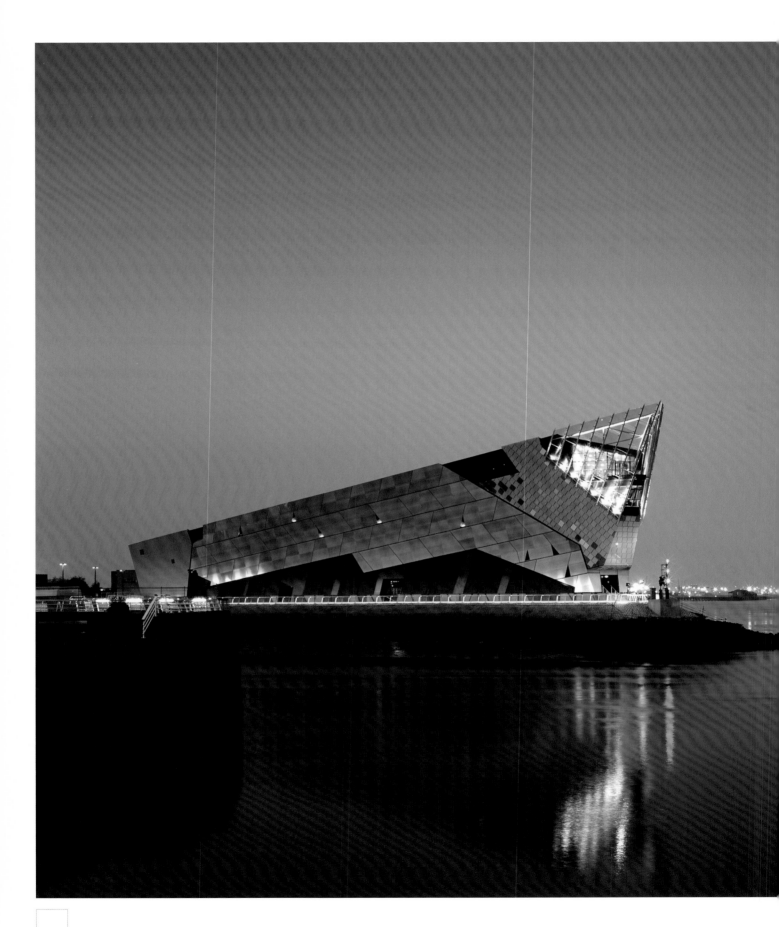

Left: The Deep, Hull. On its harbour wall site, the
Deep acts as a beacon looking out to sea

SLEEP

There's something almost sacred about children's sleep. Babies seem to take their sleep as if in unconscious dialogue with a part of themselves unknown to us. They need only a quiet well ventilated room, their cot and their mobile – their blurred vision does not need stimulation, only quiet. I have a friend who slept in a drawer when he was a baby. (Not that I recommend this – it's just that the very young need only the cocoon of their parents' love and a quiet place to sleep.)

Children surrender themselves, sleep so deeply, dream so potently, and wake up so lively and refreshed it's almost as if they are brand new along with

Sleep

the day. Parents want to guard sleep and its precious dreams – not just for their children's sake, but for their own – and so a child's bedroom is a very important place. Many bedrooms double as play rooms, so while they need to have a peaceful, simple, streamlined feel they usually also have to house toys, books, clothes, teddies and the day's treasures with relative ease. They need to be well lit – without trailing wires. Sufficient light for reading by, night lights, day lighting when skies are overcast. Bedtime, with its stories, cuddles and lullabies is a time of transition – sloughing off the day and slipping into sleep. Imaginations roam with the stories and the talk, but the surroundings need to be soothing enough, safe enough, to vanquish worries or excitement. A bedroom is a place of safety. It's important for the child to feel, 'This is my room, my private place, my domain'. And if going to bed is something to look forward to, that's a very good thing for grown-ups keen to start their evening and have their own private time.

So many stories deal with that precarious time of sleep, when children are somehow beyond their parents' reach. There's Peter Pan's snatching of Wendy, John and Michael from their nursery at bedtime; there are the fairy

Left: For young children waking in a comforting environment is important whether at home, at nursery or during a hospital stay.

Above: The Luginsland Kindergarten in Stuttgart – designed by Behnisch, Behnisch & Partner – provides a cosy place for naps in a quiet alcove off the main space.

stories of witches coming and taking children when they are asleep. I think these stories from the collective unconscious show that sleep's threshold can be like an adventure for children – they are about to embark in their dream boats – while for adults, there is an element of anxiety: they are giving the care of the children into the unknown until the next day. Anxiety, relief, love and dreams – just your average bedtime.

This chapter features some very different ideas about bedrooms. The bedroom, playroom and bathroom spaces in the basement of the family house in Kensington are very much interior designed. They are themed: the nautical bathroom, the cowboys and Indians bedroom. This might not be to everyone's taste, but it is beautifully done. The murals are simple and bold, the furniture wooden and sturdy. There isn't a feeling of a stage set, but of a real room, and there is still enough neutrality in the colours and gentle texture in the materials for the rooms to be welcoming for the very young. If I were a little lad I think I would be so happy with those bunk beds. You can actually climb on them. The room is an adventure, but soothing nonetheless. This is partly to do with proportion, but it looks so easy, just effortless good taste.

The children's bedrooms in Notting Hill, Kensington's trendier neighbour, are both more neutral and more of a statement. First, there is the feeling of the interconnectedness of the spaces – bedroom, playroom, bedroom – which comes from the three-quarter-height walls-cum-storage units. This is thoughtful. You can lie in bed and see your sibling; you can feel private in your own space and yet not cut off. Similarly, the oval peep holes are fun to climb in and out of, or just to lounge and hang out in. And there is enough storage to satisfy even the tidiest parent. There is very little colour, and what there is is strong, but there is a lot of natural light. And there is room to be creative – plenty of floor space. The nod to the '60s in the oval shapes and Retro furniture is for grown-ups only – but it doesn't jar.

In the Toronto house, the architect has simplified the spaces so much you can't really call them rooms. The advantage of the lakeside location is the

Below: In his room for his son, architect Jan Kaplicky of Future Systems chose to turn convention on its head, while also producing a room fit for a boy. He selected a full vibrant pink and designd a chrome bed for play and sleep. The strong modern lines are broken up by the lived-in clutter of toys.

Right: Incorporating a bold yachting theme, this traditional 'decorated' boy's bedroom by Laura Ashley is colourful and warm, but quite at odds with Jan Kaplicky's modernist vision.

abundance of light. And with a palette of only warm whites, the architect has – like Monet – painted with light. It floods; it forms pools; it delineates; it gives a sense of clarity and beauty. The built-in bunk-bed seems not to interfere with the space at all, similarly the storage. So what is left is just the airy room to fill with whatever games or occupation suits the child. It is a very bold room, at the same time very peaceful. It must be so calm to fall asleep in and, once you have abandoned preconceptions about Minimalism and its coldness, you can see that it's really quite a nurturing space.

No child is happy to be ill. And, usually, any more company in the bedroom than a sibling's is well outside the experience of most young children. But this is the challenge for the architects of the Evangelina Wing at St Thomas's Hospital, London. The place needs to be soothing, comforting. There must be enough feeling of privacy for relaxing sleep, but also state-of-the-art connection to the nurses, doctors, carers and visiting parents. And in practical terms, sufficient space for hospital equipment, mobile units and so on. The plans for this hospital show the architects' sensitivity to all these factors, and a tremendous sense of space and light.

We cannot prescribe the sleep our children have. But we can make conditions as right for them as possible. My son sleeps in my old study, surrounded by my books and his, his toys and my writing desk, on the walls the huge roses and hummingbird wallpaper I chose for my work room. He loves the flowers and birds. He doesn't feel cheated because he doesn't have racing cars on the walls. He has his lamplight, his toys, his little white bed with the covers embroidered with stars and he is content. They are happy when they know they are loved.

Private Bedroom and Bathroom Floor, Kensington, London

Todhunter Earle

Client: Private Client
Completion Date: 2002

These rooms are themed and set-dressed in a wonderful way. They feel authentic: cosy, yet spacious; designed, but as if they had always been there.

There is something very simple and very romantic about these rooms. They are bold in conception without being overwhelming.

The place is the semi-basement floor in the Kensington house of a professional couple with two children, one is three and the other a baby, and this is part of their suite of rooms.

In the American Indian bedroom, French windows give out onto a terrace that provides a sense of possibility and an ambient light. The bunk beds really do look as though they could have been built for a cowboy in his cabin next to the barn and stables on a ranch – they are strong, and without the saccharine detailing found on so much children's furniture. They are as solid as an outdoor timber climbing frame, robust. They even look weather resistant. The choice of fabrics at the window and on the bed is very much in subdued good taste, North America's version of the Wild West via Ralph Lauren. The room suggests feminine opulence and restraint, but it's still firmly aimed at a little boy.

The wigwam mural is all complementary earth tones – subtle yet substantial looking. It doesn't leap out at you. And the trailing curtains and rustic floor are all part of the look. It is very much a look and very styled, but practical too. And it leaves plenty for the imagination to add. It is also grown-up enough to last until the little boy is at least ten or eleven – there is nothing babyish about it. It looks strong enough to survive a good few bouts of cowboys and Indians; ideal for the rough and tumble of boys everywhere.

Giving the sailor bathroom floor-to-ceiling sliding doors is a very clever way of converting what was a dark and dingy cubbyhole into a bathroom – maximising the space, height and the use of clean lines. It is just so inviting to pull back the sailor sliding doors and have this gorgeous bath to swim about in. If I were a little boy, I couldn't wait to get into the bath. Yet all the Modernist credentials are here – from minimalist bathroom fittings to concealed storage.

These rooms are as magical for a child as a stage set come to life.

Opposite: Private Bedroom and Bathroom Floor, London. A sliding door connects wigwam room to bathroom – a generous feeling of space

Above: **Private Bedroom and Bathroom Floor, London.** Size matters. The huge scale of the sailing boat mural that covers the bedroom cupboards – like something out of C. S. Lewis – and the large sliding doors, between bedroom and bathroom, disguise the latter's tinyness

Opposite: **Private Bedroom and Bathroom Floor, London.** The cowboy room, with its purpose-built bunk-beds

Family House, Toronto, Canada

Seth Stein Architects

Client: Private Client
Completion Date: December 1999

Like a living ice sculpture animated by light, movement and, of course, people, this house cannot fail to stun an observer. It gives the concept of clean living new meaning. For a small child, space is provided to fill with activity and play, free of clutter and objects, and with a restrained use of colour.

This really is the most extraordinary house. Built on the edge of a ravine in a suburban area in Toronto, it presents four interlocking courtyards to its public street side, while the façade that faces the ravine is almost entirely made of glass. The light in this part of the world is very pale and bright even in winter, so the way it enters the house and how it is used in the interior is a major element in the impression of an almost glowing whiteness and abstract form.

Inside, it's almost sculptural, making use of wall planes and cylinders. Where photographs may lend it a kind of icy Modernist aura, in real life, the house is said to be warm and welcoming. Much of its life and warmth relies on the play of light that is difficult to capture on film.

The main spaces open one into another, providing constant vistas and a sense of expansiveness. This is in many ways ideal for family life, because no room is cut off from another, and the living space is open and accessible from all parts of the house. Each child has their own space, connected by bridges and walkways. The storage units are enormous. There is absolutely no clutter. When you're living in a sculpture you really can't have Telly Tubbies lying around.

There is tremendous attention to detail – all the walls stop just short of the floor for that perfect shadow gap and there is nothing decorative. There is a system of louvred skylights, and areas of colour, including indigo and a beautiful block of pink which is floodlit at night to be visible from the kitchen window. The white walls are a carefully chosen warm off-white to create a generous feel without the grey blue tones of brilliant white.

One child's bedroom has the most amazing bunk bed cum storage unit which looks like something futuristic. It has all the ingredients for fun: a hidden lower bunk that looks like an ice cave; exciting steps complete with handrail for climbing to the top bunk, which has a strategically placed window above it. The little dinosaur skeleton emphasises the extraordinary pared-

Above: **Family House, Toronto.** Here you can see the elegance of the way this house is conceived

Above: **Family House, Toronto.** These bunk-beds are as simple as a sculpture, blending seamlessly with the room, as if they've grown out of it. It's very elegant and there's plenty of room for a train set

down quality of the space. One can only hope that this clarity of approach really appeals to the children and doesn't make them feel as if they are in a middle of a snow desert.

The second bedroom looks rather less inviting – a vast cylinder of storage space and a high clerestory window. There's a toy up there in the window, so I imagine you can climb up there and somehow reach it, which would be great fun.

Pared-down treatments for children are a matter of taste. But an under five might just respond positively to this house. Unrestricted clean space for self-expression, or cramping perfectionism? Or even a little bit of both? Whatever your opinion, it's an inspiring building, conceived and executed with precision and style.

Right: **Family House, Toronto.** Although Minimalism has been around a long time, this still has the shock of the new. Where there was clutter let there be a cylinder and a small plastic pram

Left: Evelina Children's Hospital, London. The children's outpatients area with the helter skelter and centrally placed lifts

Above: Evelina Children's Hospital, London.
View of the building from Lambeth Palace Park

Right: Evelina Children's Hospital, London.
The natural light-filled ward – the clerestory window
connects one space to another to give a feeling of
generosity. You can see the sea motif on the floor
and a pull-out bed next to the cot

Left: Private Playroom and Bedrooms, London.
Discreet, accessible and abundant storage.
You can see each child's bed through its own
oval cuddle space-cum-climbing frame

Above: **Private Playroom and Bedrooms, London.**
Sight lines in the space are varied and playful

Below: **Private Playroom and Bedrooms, London.**
This must be such fun to play and relax in

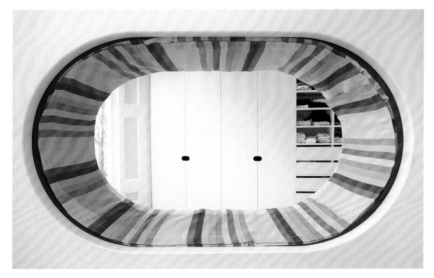

Above: **Private Playroom and Bedrooms, London.**
Bedroom and playspace: seemingly effortlessly
connected

Listing of Public Places

American Museum of
Natural History
Central Park West at 79th Street
New York
NY 10024 5912
T (1) 212 769 5100

Babington House
Babington
nr Frome
Somerset BA11 3RW
T 01373 812 266
F 01373 812 112
enquiries@babingtonhouse.co.uk
www.babingtonhouse.co.uk

Blue Kangaroo
555 Kings Road
London SW6 2EB
T 020 7371 7622
www.thebluekangaroo.co.uk

The Deep
Hull HU1 4DP
T 01482 381000
F 01482 381018
info@thedeep.co.uk
www.thedeep.co.uk

London Aquarium
County Hall
Westminster Bridge Road
London SE1 7PB
T 020 7967 8000
F 020 7967 8029
info@londonaquarium.co.uk
www.londonaquarium.co.uk

Discover Children's Centre
1 Bridge Terrace
Stratford
London E15 4BG
T 020 8536 5555
www.discover.org.uk

Dulwich Picture Gallery
Gallery Road
Dulwich Village
London SE21 7AD
T 020 8693 5254
www.dulwichpicturegallery.org.uk

Museum of Childhood
Cambridge Heath Road
London E2 9PA
T 020 8983 5200
F 020 8983 5225
www.museumofchildhood.org.uk

Pavilions in the Park
Hurst Road
Horsham Park
Horsham
T 01403 219 200
F 01403 219 203
enquiries@thepavilionsinthepark.co.uk
www.horsham.co.uk/atlantis

Peckham Library
122 Peckham Hill Street
London SE15 5JR
T 020 7525 0200
F 020 7525 0202

Roald Dahl Children's Gallery
Bucks County Museum
Church Street
Aylesbury HP20 2QP
T 01296 331 441

Royal Botanic Gardens
Kew
Richmond upon Thames
Surrey TW9 3AB
T 020 8332 5655
info@kew.org
www.kew.org/climbersandcreepers

Science Museum
Exhibition Road
South Kensington
London SW7 2DD
T 0870 870 4868
www.sciencemuseum.org.uk

Tresanton Hotel
Lower Castle Road
St Mawes
Cornwall TR2 4DR
T 01326 270055
F 01326 270053
info@tresanton.com
www.tresanton.com

Listing of Architects

Adams & Sutherland
Studio 1K
Highgate Business Centre
33 Greenwood Place
London NW5 1LB
T 020 7267 1747
F 020 7482 2359
info@adams-sutherland.co.uk
www.adams-sutherland.co.uk

AHMM Ltd
2nd Floor
Block B
Morelands
5-23 Old Street
London EC1V 9HL
T 020 7251 5261
info@ahmm.co.uk

Alsop Architects
Bishops Wharf
34-39 Parkgate Road
London SW11 4NP
T 020 7978 7878
F 020 7978 7879
walsop@alsoparchitects.com
www.alsoparchitects.com

Behnisch, Behnisch & Partner
Rotebühlstrasse 163A
70197 Stuttgart
Germany
T (49) 0711 607 720
F (49) 0711 607 7299
www.behnisch.com

Bremner & Orr Design
Consultants Ltd
The Garden Studios
53-55 Long Street
Tetbury
Glos. GL8 8AA
T 01666 503007

Caruso St John Architects
1 Coate Street
London E2 9AG
T 020 7613 3161
F 020 7729 6188
info@carusostjohn.com
www.carusostjohn.com

The Children's Cottage Company
The Sanctuary
Shobrooke
Crediton
Devon EX17 1BG
01363 772061
www.play-houses.com

CR Studio Architects PC
6 West 18th Street
9th Floor
New York
NY 10011
T (1) 313 989 8187
www.crstudio.com

Dannatt, Johnson Architects
52c Borough High Street
London SE1 1XN
T 020 7357 7100
www.djarchitects.co.uk

Denise Ho Architects
Room 205
Chit Lee Commercial Building
30-36 Shaukeiwan Road
Hong Kong
T (852) 2884 2815
denhoarc@netvigator.com

Dragons of Walton Street
23 Walton Street
Knightsbridge
London SW3 2HX
T: 020 7589 3795
www.dragonsofwaltonstreet.com

Drost + van Veen Architecten
Pieter de Hoochweg 18
3024 BH Rotterdam
T (31) 010 477 49 64
architecten@drostvanveen.nl

dsdha
8 Iliffe Yard
London SW17 3QA
T 020 7703 3555
F 020 7703 3890
info@dsdha.co.uk

FaulknerBrowns
7th Floor
52 Grosvenor Gardens
London SW1W
T 020 7931 0954
F 020 7681 1036
email@faulknerbrowns.co,uk
www.faulknerbrowns.co.uk

Future Systems
The Warehouse
20 Victoria Gardens
London W11 3PE
T 020 7243 7670
F 020 7243 7690
email@future-systems.com
www.future-systems.com

Gans & Jelacic
350 Fifth Avenue
Suite 8006
New York
New York 10118
T (1) 212 643 8575
office@gansandjelacic.com

Gehry Partners
12541 Beatrice Street
Los Angeles
CA 90066-7001
T (1) 310 482 3000
F (1) 310 482 3006

Hawkins Brown Architects
60 Bastwick Street
London EC1V 3TN
T 020 7336 8030
www.hawkinsbrown.co.uk

Hopkins Architects
27 Broadley Terrace
London NW1 6LG
T 020 7724 1751
F 020 7723 0932
mail@hopkins.co.uk
www.hopkins.co.uk

Joan Rodon Arquitectes Associats
Camp 64
08022 Barcelona
T (34) 093 254 1570
F (34) 093 418 7614
www.rodonarquitecte.es

Michaelis Boyd Associates Ltd
90a Notting Hill Gate
London W11 3HPP
T 020 72211237
F 020 72210130
www.michaelisboyd.com

RHWL
77 Endell Street
London W11 3HPP
T 020 7221 1237
F 020 7221 0130
www.rhwl.com

Rick Mather
123 Camden High Street
London NW1 7JR
T 020 7284 1727
www.rickmather.com

Seth Stein Architects
15 Grand Union Centre
West Row
Ladbroke Grove
London W10 5AS
T 020 8968 8581
F 020 8968 8591
www.sethstein.com

Terry Farrell & Partners
7 Hatton Street
London NW8 8PL
T 020 7258 3433
F 020 7723 7059
enquiries@terryfarrell.co.uk
www.terryfarrell.co.uk

Terry Pawson
206 Merton High Street
London SW19 1AY
T 020 8543 2577
F 020 8543 8677
tpa@terrypawson.com
www.terrypawson.com

Todhunter Earle Ltd
Chelsea Reach
1st Floor
79-89 Lots Road
London SW10 0RN
T 020 7349 9999
F 020 7349 0410
interiors@todhunterearle.com

Walters & Cohen
Studio 420
Highgate Studios
53–79 Highgate Road
London NW5 1TL
T 020 7428 9751
F 020 7428 9752
mail@waltersandcohen.com
www.waltersandcohen.com

Wilkinson Eyre Architects
Transworld House
100 City Road
London EC1Y 2BP
T 020 7608 7900
www.wilkinsoneyre.com

Bibliography

The following books were useful in my research:

Kroner, Walter, *Architecture for Children*, Kramer, Stuttgart/Zurich, 1994

This book showcases kindergartens and is useful for its ideas on providing for children in the right way: safety, colour, the durability of materials, storage, play space, outside space, energy efficiency, and the planning of kitchens and bathrooms.

Matrix, *Building for Childcare*, Matrix and GLC Women's Cooperative, London, 1986

A short book, very much of its time, and deeply feminist. Discusses the needs of children and their families. It does not take an aesthetic approach.

Le Corbusier (ed), *Nursery Schools*, Orion Press, New York, 1968

This small book by Le Corbusier describes the genesis of the school at the Unité d'Habitation in Marseilles. Illustrated with drawings and photographs, a hand-drawn pie-chart to show the division of children's time and embellished with quotes from Mme Ongier – who created the school – among others, the book is a record of the realisation of a dream, not just of a building but a way of life and community. Profoundly subjective.

Kindergarten Architecture, Loft Publications, London, 2001

This book is a fantastic showcase for kindergarten architecture, mainly European. It is highly illustrated with exceptional photographs and provides an interesting record of contrasting approaches and styles. Text not in English.

Dudek, Mark, *Kindergarten Architecture: Space for the Imagination*, Spon Press, London, 2000

This book provided most of the background information on the development of the kindergarten, and facts and figures about present-day childcare. It is diligently researched and extremely informative, as well as thought-provoking.

The following books are widely available UK or US publications about adapting the domestic space for children. They focus on the home, interior design and decoration, including DIY, rather than looking at an interior as a whole architectural space. Well illustrated and full of useful ideas:

Creative Spaces for Kids, Octopus (Hamlyn), London, 2002

Copestick, Joanna, *Children's Rooms, Practical Design Solutions 0–10*, Conran Octopus, London, 2002

Gilchrist, Paige, *Rooms Your Kids will Love*, Lark Books, 2002

Jordan, Wendy, *Taunton's Kidspace Ideas Book*, 2002

Kasabian, Anna, *Kids' Rooms: A Hands-on Decorating Guide*, Rockport, 2001

Santiesteban, Eugenia, *Living with Kids*, Rockport, 2003

Wilson, Judith, *Children's Spaces 0–10*, Ryland Peters & Small, 2001

Scheffler, Carol, *Great Kids' Rooms*, Sterling Publishing, 2004